TOKYO
FLOWERS

Yuji Kobayashi

TOKYO
FLOWERS

Yuji Kobayashi

stichting
kunstboek

YUJI KOBAYASHI

Tokyo is a city influenced by various cultures, rapidly changing and evolving every day. Information goes around the world very fast these days, and wherever we are, we can share the exact same information simultaneously. Our flower industry is no exception. Consumers are well informed, and the highly improved distribution system allows them to purchase flowers online quite easily. Everyone has access to high quality flowers, less expensive flowers, and even rare imported flowers if they wish. Furthermore, with the recent prevalence of preserved flowers, we, floral designers, are challenged to reconsider the core value and possibilities of arrangement work with fresh flowers as a creative art form.

When decorating with flowers, we select the plant material extremely carefully in terms of its suitability, taking into consideration such factors as the venue for the display, the occasion and the plant material's nature. We collaborate with the plant material, considering its individual look, reflection, character, and even its emotional expression.
In TOKYO FLOWERS, I have managed to have the

plants work harmoniously with my own creative ideas, by analyzing their characteristics, having conversations with them repeatedly and watching carefully for their reactions. That having been said, most plants were very stubborn and having my way was never easy. However, in the end, the plants always showed us their most beautiful expression. But therefore we had to clarifiy our design for each arrangement and try to express it to and with the flowers.

In my opinion, flower arranging is combining artificial and natural beauty and displaying the overlapping portion. Flower design has its guilty side as we sometimes manipulate the plant material ignoring how they naturally grow and live. Therefore, we must always be respectful to the plants in our design work, since they are living creatures and their lives are in our hands.

I've always wanted the plants to be highlighted as 'a whole world' in a photographic collection focusing on the endless possibilities of their beauty, and not treat them as a part of an interior

concept or any other design. In this book,
this idea has been realized.
I hope you feel the true beauty of each stem of
plant, and if you capture the moment where the
identities of the flowers and my own creativity are
flowing together harmoniously in these pages,
I will be very happy.

I'm certain I shall go on living with flowers,
wishing for many more opportunities to
collaborate with them, willing to face them
with uncompromising creativity and artistry to
bring out their natural beauty to the maximum.
Hoping this would play a small role for Tokyo, our
beautiful city to flourish further more.

Yuji Kobayashi

SHAPE OF
ARRANGEMENTS

On this earth, there are countless varieties of plants ranging from a dainty flower blooming sweetly in the fields to a bulbous plant with a thick stem perhaps five centimeters in diameter. There are plants in most peculiar shapes, and even those we feel familiar with and seem simple are actually quite complex. When looking close enough, we will realize that the size and the positioning of flower petals or leaves have precise, almost mathematical patterns. There is no question that plants simply exist to preserve their species, just like any other living creature. Their beauty, giving us so much pleasure is never their primal objective. The individual colors and structures were formed by their own genetic program in the process of evolution and that miraculous power of nature is most astonishing.

Our life is becoming more and more design-orientated. The huge increase in lifestyle accessories is a good example. Also, graphic design tends to be further appreciated in the interior design world. In our lifestyle, including fashion, individuality is more respected and

designs with distinct color and style are preferred. When decorating for occasions or places with specific themes, we need to show our originality in a quite restrained way. We are required to have the flexibility and technique to execute the arrangement in a style and way most appropriate for the opportunity. In a natural style on one occasion and in an artificial style for another.

When we want a floral design concept that is geometrical with straight and curved lines, it is crucial to choose suitable flowers. In our flower arrangements, we usually use the standardized plant material available on the market, only on rare occassions we create designs using flowers blooming randomly in the fields. The plants growing in the fields absorbing sunshine and thermal energy give us a strong impression of their enormous vitality. On the contrary, the decorative plants cultivated for the market have 'perfectly' straight stems. With some addition and changes to their nature, the original fairly straight stems have been improved. In other words, the decorative plants in the market have already been made artificial before they even reach our hands. Their shape is made artificial long before we acquire them, so we may say that geometric floral designs are merely an extension of that process. What does arranging flowers into solid geometric shapes mean? In my opinion, the formal geometric arrangement is a design where the outline is crystal-clear and the shape can easily be described in words. In contrast, in traditional arrangements the overall outline is kept vague and that's precisely where its vitality, natural beauty and contentment lies.

At the extreme opposite, our arrangements are conceptual and demand an opinion from those who encounter it. Like the sensation we feel when facing skyscrapers in an international city, a feeling of tension can build up when facing the arrangement and one may even feel restless or uncomfortable. Neither style is better than the other.

Both styles are significant and useful for floral design. It is necessary to carefully choose the appropriate style depending on the purpose of each arrangement.

When working on a geometric arrangement, the idea of a dominant shape becomes clearer when considering the compatibility of the arrangement with containers or candles and its harmony with the surrounding area. The relationship between flowers and equipment is extremely delicate. When too many items are surrounding the arrangement, the look and the purpose of the decoration could be killed, being unable to emphasize the 'live' aspect of the plants. Using candles can be highly effective in some cases, but they may also become excessively appealing, demanding too much attention, and disturb the presence of the flowers. In my signature design, when using candles in glass containers, I try to achieve the best balance between flowers and candles within the geometrical design by positioning them in ways that do not draw too much attention. As they are made of far different material than the plants, the layout of the candles and the effect of their light - which is quite eye-catching - has to be taken into consideration when thinking of visual balance. Candle light is a natural light and therefore goes well with plants without giving an out of place impression. Still, we should never forget the risks of fire and always keep sufficient distance between the candles and plants to assure safety. Once these criteria are met, the flowers will show and surprise us with their different attractive faces reflecting the light.

When we have a commission for an event, we usually have a meeting with the client for further information. The main concept for the event, the period in which it is held, the conditions of the venue and the availability of air conditioning system (depending on the season),... is vital information. After visiting and checking the venue, we have a meeting with the supplier from the flower market to make sure all the details of the plant materials are just right. As the venue has tables with food and flowers, all calculated, positioned and precisely planned, one cannot neglect the exact size of the plant material. In case of producing a geometric arrangement, any differences in the numerous flowers arriving from the market in terms of the size of flower

heads and length or thickness of stems could be fatal. It would be quite difficult to shape the exact figure of arrangement with flowers varying in size. It is no exaggeration to say that the work would reach a higher degree of perfection by using cloned flowers.

Once the flowers that will be used in the arrangements are decided on, I start drawing plans and rough sketches. The size of each arrangement is determined depending on the setting for the decoration and its sketch is drawn in reduced size on paper, as accurately as possible to avoid ambiguous design. It is crucial to keep the on-site working time to a minimum particularly at a large-scale event, as these events involve a large number of arrangements and flowers that have to stay fresh. Sharing those sketches makes it possible for each team member to start with different tasks at the same time and to achieve remarkable efficiency. Therefore the preliminary meeting is extremely important and going over all details in advance takes up an equal amount of time as the actual arrangement work. Leading a project entirely based on personal inspiration is not my style. Consequently we hardly see any substantial differences between the original rough sketch and the finished work, although, as a matter of fact, we add minor changes to the initial plan during the working process to bring it closer to the goal we aim to achieve.

In TOKYO FLOWERS, I classified the arrangements into groups according to their geometrical shape. The basic formal style with flowers in straight lines and the more advanced styles, variations on the basic figures, have been included in those groups. I could have classified them into even smaller groups or categories, but I chose not.

Flowers have phenomenal strength. Even one flower may have enough power to heal us and sometimes that is all we need. However, I hope to see how the flowers react to our expectations, to the unknown and to our creativity.

With highest regard to the plants.

SQUARE

Flowers naturally have curved rather than straight lines, forming shapes and structures best adapted to survival on earth. Thus, when creating a square arrangement with curvy plant material, we should note the following.

Firstly, make sure the general size of the arrangement and the size of the plant material to be used is compatible. Choose flowers most suitable for the decoration, taking into consideration the amount of space necessary to allow each flower to look its best.

Secondly, create flat surfaces with flowers. Since a difference in width and height of each flower head creates unevenness, use at least a row of seven flowers to assure flatness and maximum color.

Thirdly, always make sharp corners. This can be achieved by using a suitable amount of plant material and by placing the flowers with pinpoint accuracy. This also brings desirable tension to the arrangement.

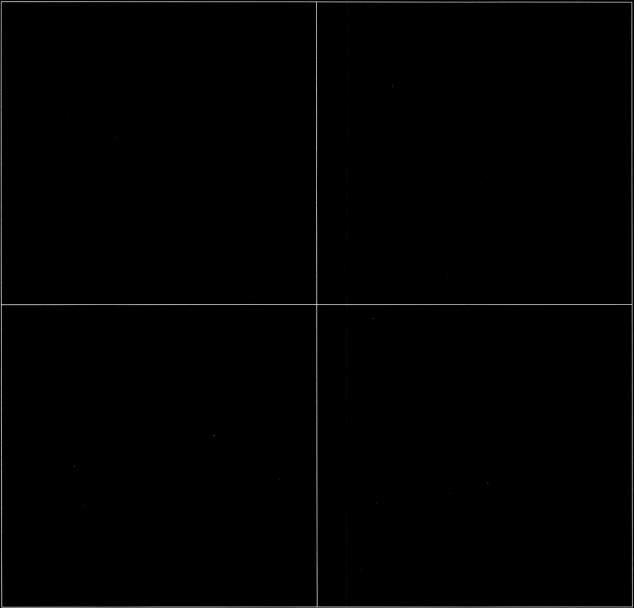

ICHIMATSU MOYO (CHECKERS)

Ichimatsu moyo (or checker pattern) was popular in the Edo era since it was used in the theatrical costumes of kabuki actor Sanogawa Ichimatsu. Even now, this simple pattern can be regarded as modern and we can find it in the interior designs of many rooms for events or parties. When decorating with this version of Japanese checkers, further Japanese atmosphere can be achieved by intentionally using plant materials grown in Asia.

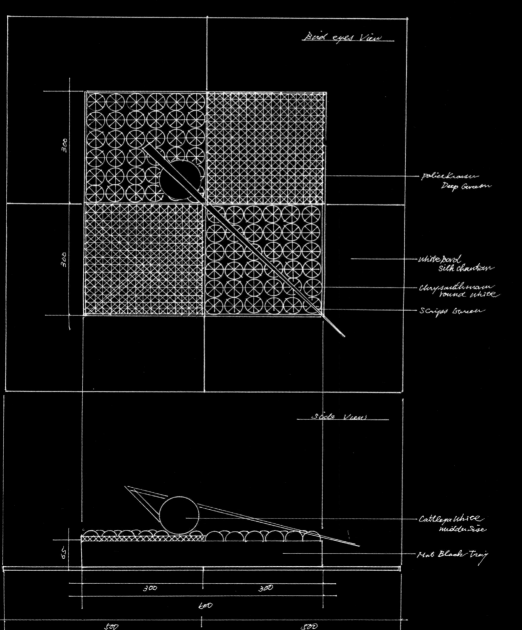

ROSEMARY

Rosemary is familiar to us as a garden plant, in a pot for instance. As the chefs at restaurants use it in their cooking, fresh rosemary is often seen in a corner of their open-style kitchens. I arranged freshly cut rosemary in stainless steel vases and put them in a row. It gives an impression modern enough for a restaurant in New York City.

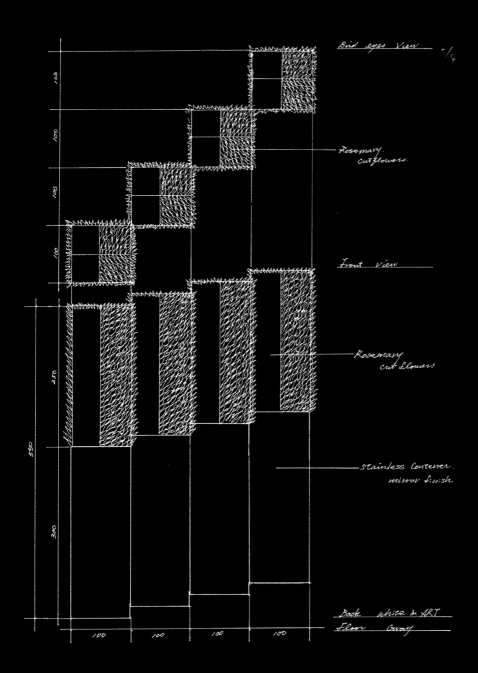

CRIMSON AMARYLLIS

The flower heads of Amaryllises are carefully removed from their stems, and several of them are stabbed and piled up on a wire, all facing upward. An appropriate amount of space should be kept between the adjacent flowers as they open widely in the same direction. It is crucial to carefully and attentively pile up the flowers as they may visually appear as just one mass of color if positioned too close to each other.

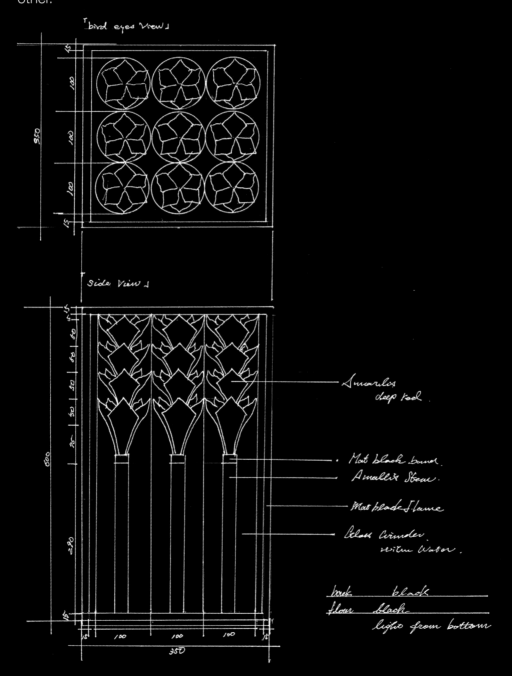

forming a mass of color, gives it a very radical impression.

as a trinity together with the two panels made of horizontal

lrush.

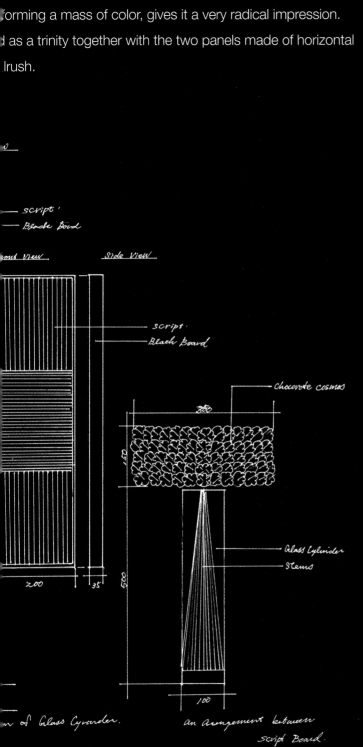

— script

— Black Board

Front View .   Side View

— script .

— Black Board

— Chocovate cosmos

350

650

200   35   500

Glass Cylinder

Stems

100

n of Glass Cylinder.   an arrangement between

script Board.

PINK (PEONY, MALLOW)

In general, pink flower material guarantees a soft and casual visual impression. For a modern and polished look, pink materials should be arranged in clearly defined lines to make them work as a basis for a geometric figure. The heads of the peonies are arranged in a row and candles are set in the middle to intensify the straightness. The outline of the mallows is clarified by the outline of the glass cylinders acting as their frame.

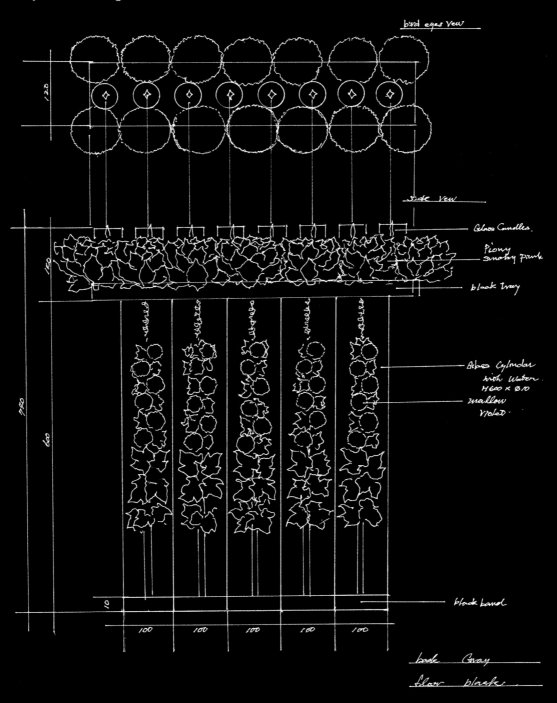

YULAN MAGNOLIA

This square arrangement was created using nothing but stems and buds of Yulan Magnolia. All stems are cut to an even length of sixty centimeters and are bent at right angles in the middle. Fairly thick wires are taped alongside the stems to achieve precise and identical angles when bending. Repeating the same procedure and taking care that all buds are even in height results in a flat top surface.

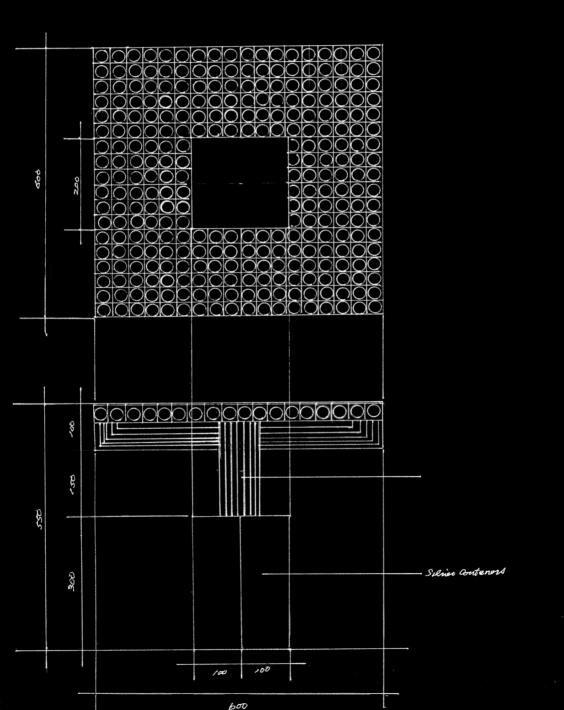

Silvia Gutenoss

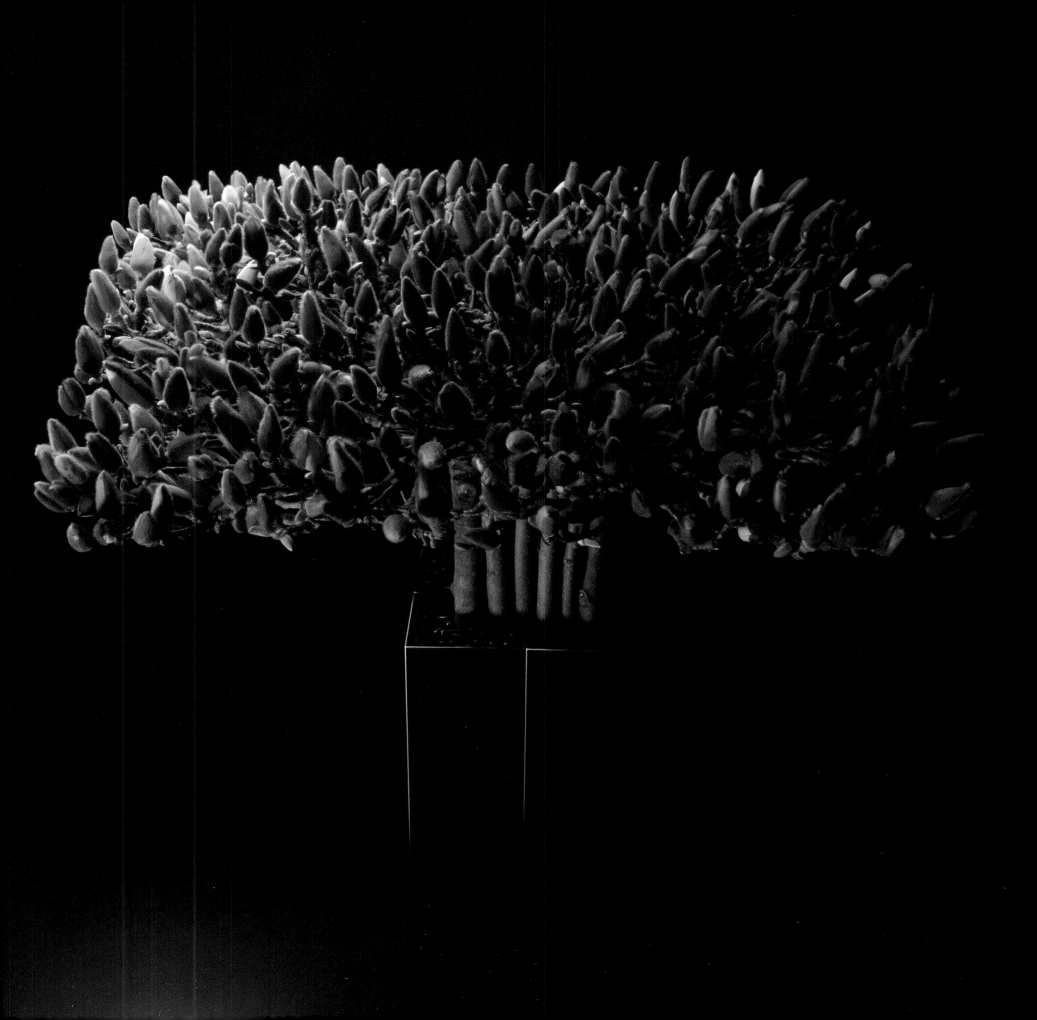

WHITE OF DEN PHAL (CAMELLIA, DEN PHAL)

Flower heads of Den Phals are taken off their stems. Since the base of the flower head is fragile and cannot be easily placed in the floral foam it is supported by wire, going into the flower head and winding down on the stem with florist's wiring technique. A flat white surface with only petals visible is created by arranging the flowers tightly, almost by squeezing them against each other.

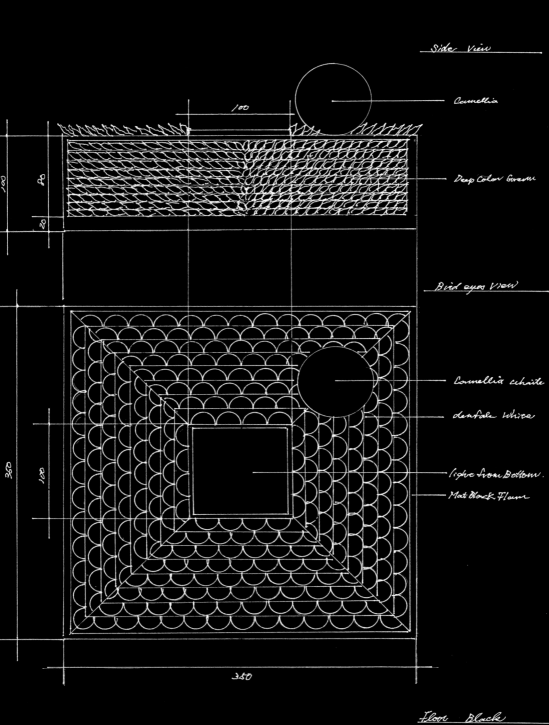

Side View

Camellia

Deep Color Given

100

90

20

Bird eyes View

Camellia white

danfale white

light from Bottom.

Mat Black Flam

350

100

350

350

Floor Black

GEOMETRIC FOLIAGE (AMAZON LILY, GREAT BULRUSH)

Foliage is rarely used as main plant material in an arrangement.
Great bulrush makes it possible to draw a precise artificial pattern if placed
well, taking advantage of its simple shape.

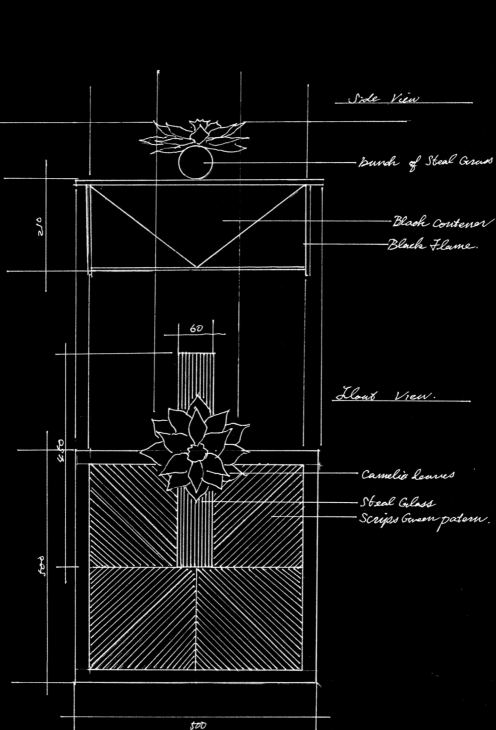

Side View

bunch of Steal Grass

Black Container
Black Flame.

Float View.

Camelia leaves
Steal Glass
Scripts Green patern.

PAPER-COVERED LAMP STAND (CYMBIDIUM, SCOURING RUSH)

The paper-covered lamp stand, made of a wooden frame, paper shade and lamp oil was used in the Edo era to light the interior of houses. Candles in glass containers are placed inside the lamp stand with a shade created out of Cymbidiums instead of traditional paper. The flowers are aligned in multiple vertical rows to form a flat square surface. The candle light softly shines through the thick flower petals of the Cymbidiums. This arrangement can be a real surprise when used as a decoration for events or parties.

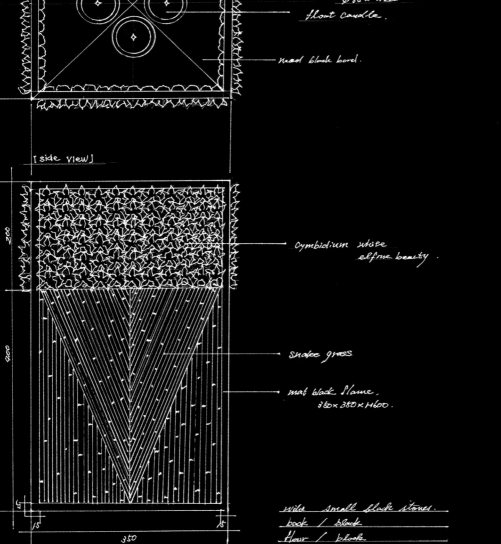

[bird eyes view]

glass Cylinder
Ø 85 × H 200

float candle.

mead black bowl.

[side view]

Cymbidium white
elfine beauty .

snake grass

mat black flame.
350 × 350 × H600.

wide small black stones.
book / black
floor / black

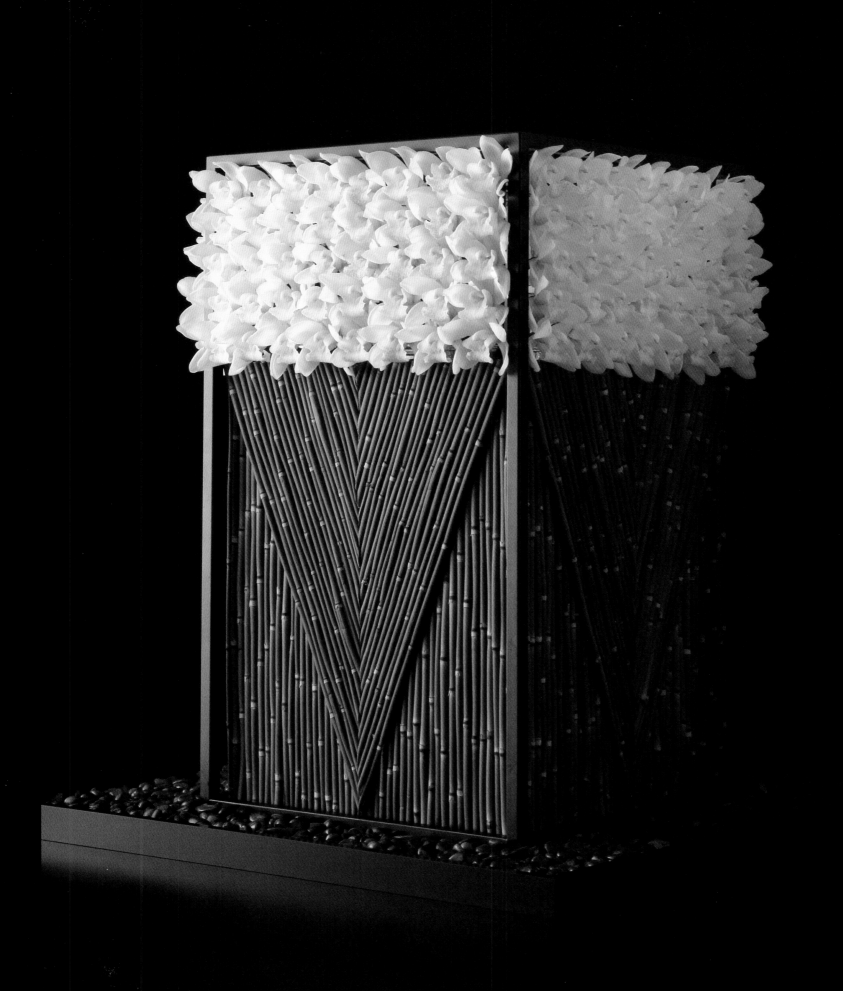

SUGITAMA

'Sugitama', an ornament made with tips of Japanese cedars, is traditionally hung at the eaves of sake breweries. It is an old custom, indicating that the new sake has been completed, as winter yields to spring. Sugitama will eventually become brown and dry, being exposed to wind and rain for a long time. Japanese link this to sake's gradual maturing. A stem of Narcissus decorated with Sugitama is a seasonal flower of early spring. Both tell us the new season has come.

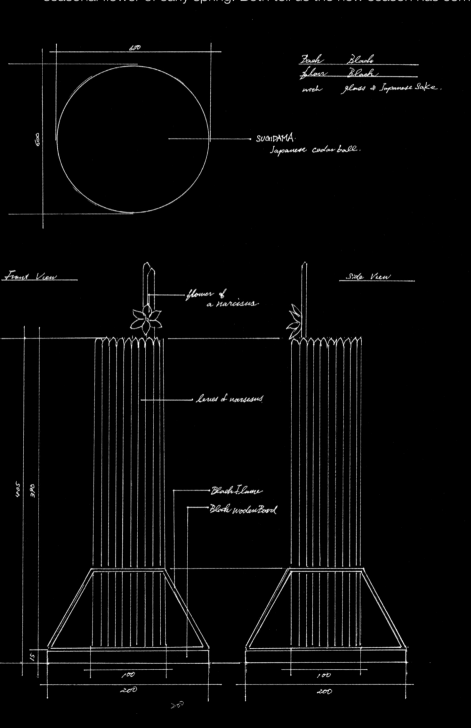

BAMBOO COMPOSITION

Using bamboo is one effective way to arrange a Japanese style floral decoration for foreign clients. Typically, they are combined with branches or flowers with an equally Japanese flavor or they are used cleaved and curved, particularly in Ikebana. My main aim in this arrangement was to show how simple and modern they could be, aligning multiple bamboos upright.

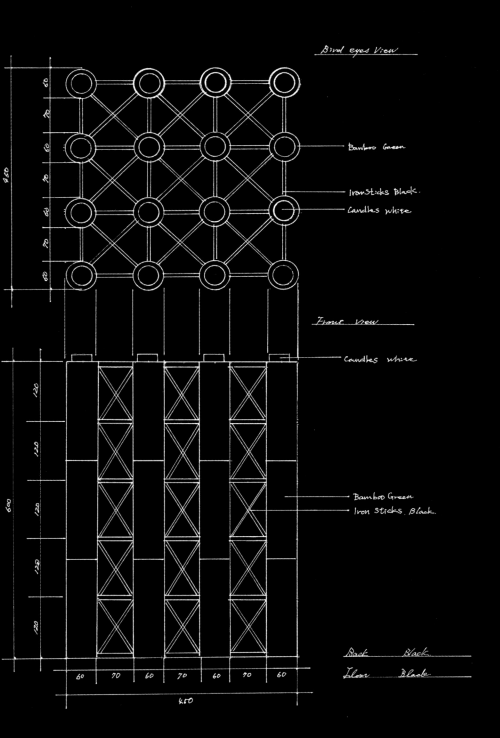

Bird eyes View

Bamboo Green

Iron Sticks Black.
Candles white

Front View

Candles white

Bamboo Green
Iron Sticks Black.

Back   Black.
Floor   Black.

RAPE

Sen No Rikyuu, a tea master during the Warring States period was a so called 'multi-producer' who left his mark in various areas, including furnishings for the tea hut and the selection of the tea service set. He was a connoisseur of a great many things. It is said that Rape was his choice of last flower when he was sentenced to death by Hideyoshi Toyotomi. Rape is also the typical decoration for hinamatsuri, a March festival celebrating young girls growing up.

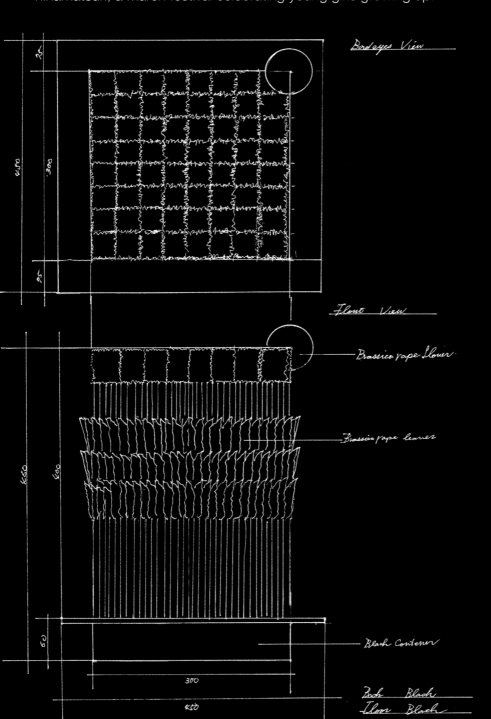

Bird eyes View

Flont View

Brassica rape flower.

Brassica rape leaves

Black Container

Body   Black
Floor   Black

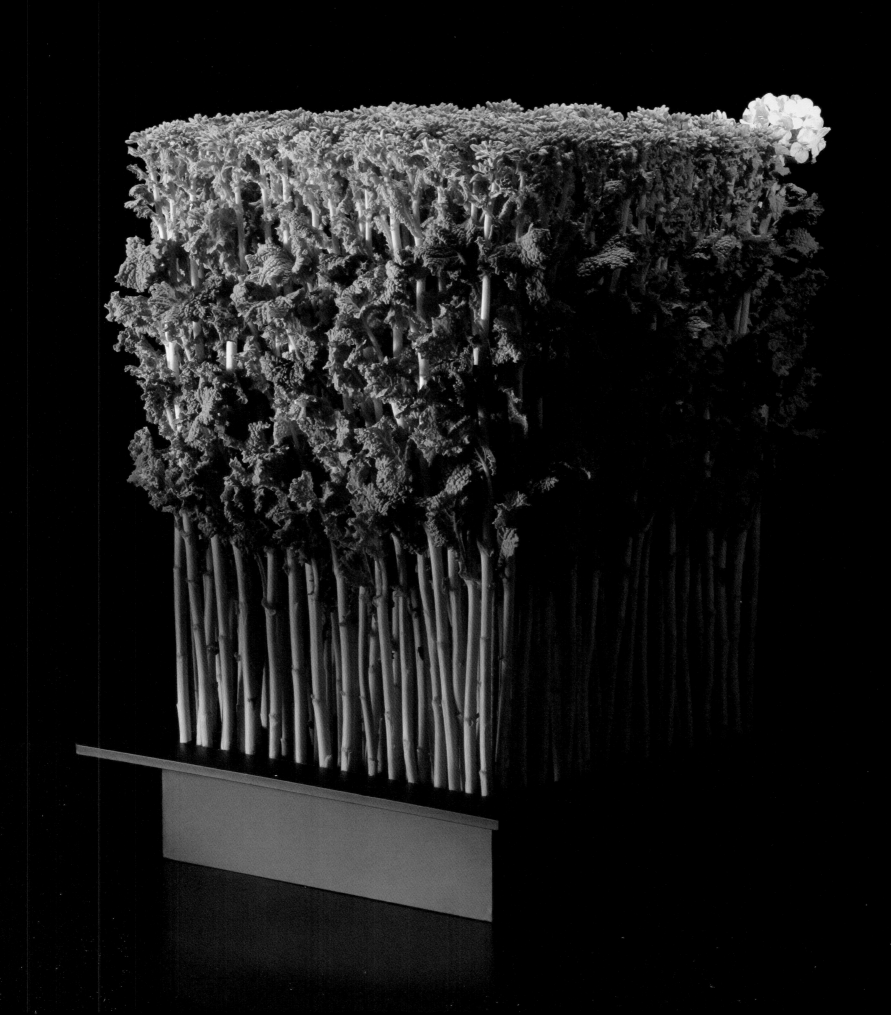

SPLENDOR OF DAHLIA

Dahlia looks most splendid when looked at from immediately above the blooming flower head, as a consequence they are mostly used for low arrangements. When creating a high arrangement using Dahlia, we raise the flowers by arranging them in multiple layers. The flowers blooming high above cannot be seen. However, by looking at them in the lower area, the viewers can easily imagine the sight of the flowers up there, which makes this arrangement possible.

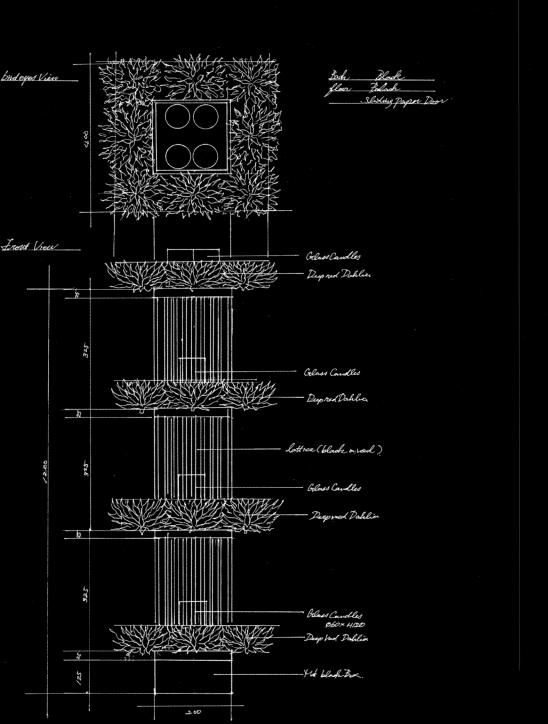

JAPANESE PLANT MATERIAL (HYDRANGEA, BAMBOO, MOSS)

Hydrangea, bamboo and moss are typical plant materials to achieve a Japanese impression. We arranged the moss in a geometric shape using a rectangular parallelepiped vase with partitions on the side, this assures a contemporary, urban look. Using bamboo and moss together in the conventional way, would make the whole arrangement look too much like a Japanese garden. As a contrast, Hydrangea and bamboo are arranged in a simple and natural way.

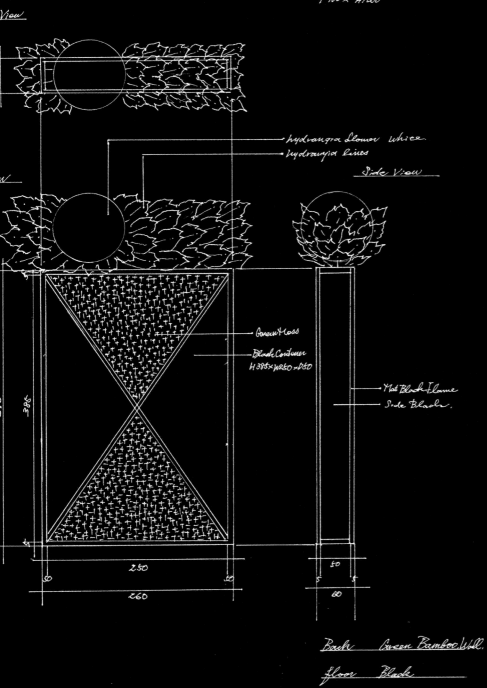

Bamboo wall from kyoto.
P 100 × H1000

View

hydrangia flower white.
hydrangia lines

Side View

Green Moss

Black Container
H 385 × W250 × D50

Mat Black Flame
Side Black.

250

50

260

80

Back   Green Bamboo Wall.

Floor   Black

REPETITIVE DECORATION (CHRYSANTHEMUM, SCOURING RUSH)

Green Chrysanthemums are placed in a rectangular parallelepiped container made of
scouring rush. A single slender container may give too simple an impression.
A stronger visual impact is achieved by a repetition of several identical arrangements.
They work well for a long dinner table in a banquet hall.

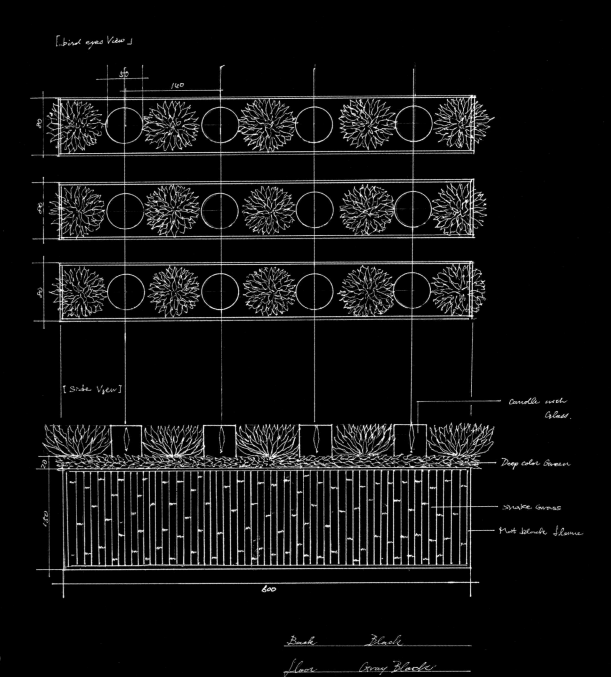

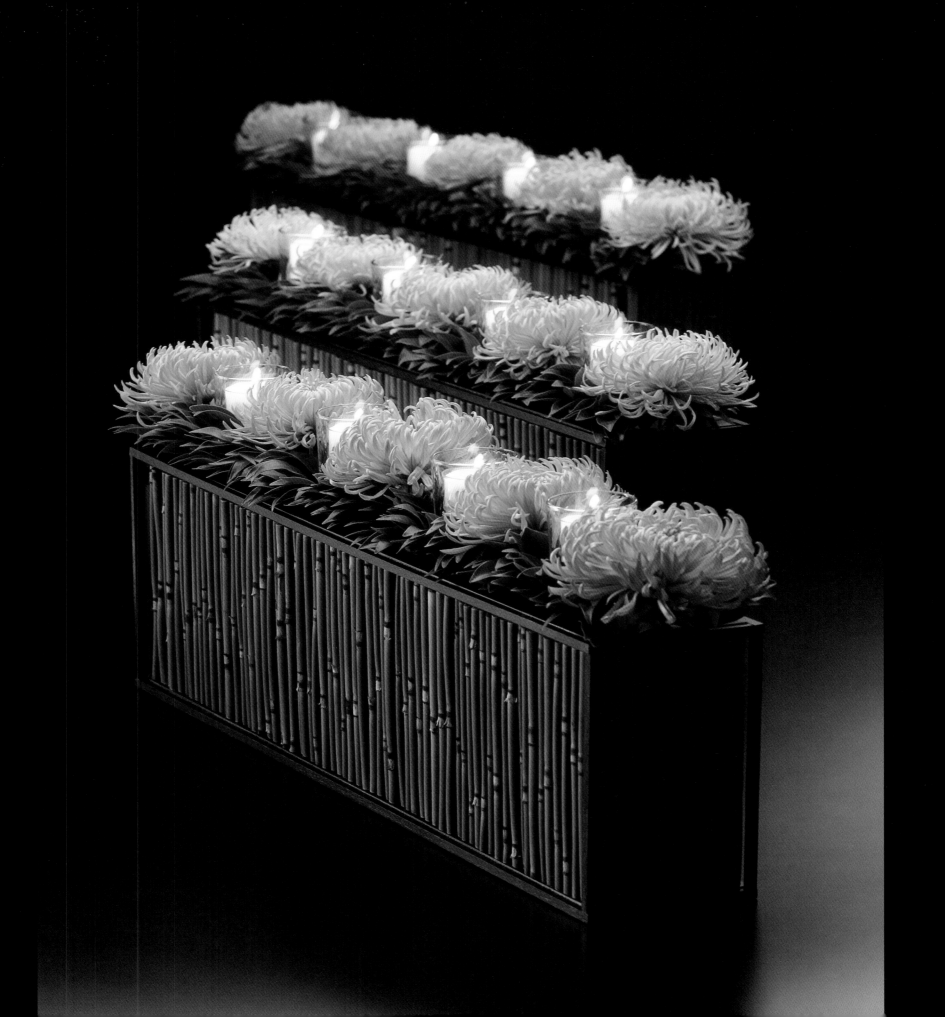

MUSCARI

Gregarious flowers of Muscari are packed tightly together in a rectangular container. In an adjacent container Muscari leaves are gathered. At first, the leaves were left full lenght which is the same height as the flowers, next they were trimmed down to a certain height, giving the arrangement an edgy finishing touch. The geometric pattern, drawn by continuous curved lines of trimmed leaves, appeared on the surface as a result.

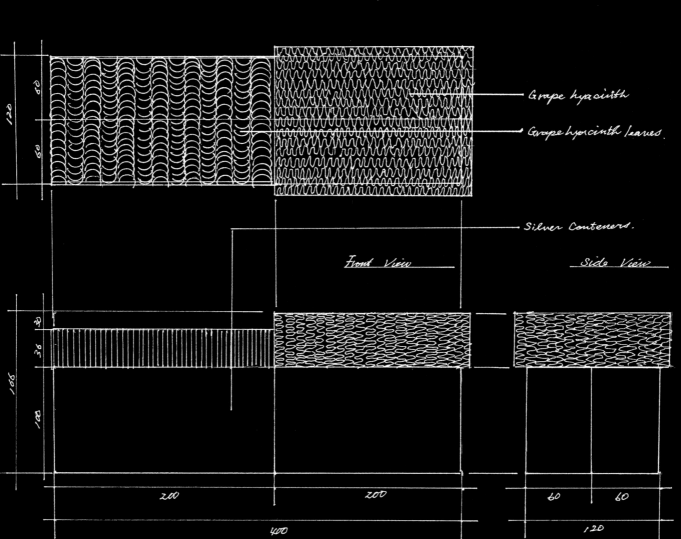

Bird eyes View

Grape hyacinth

Grape hyacinth leaves.

Silver Conteners.

Front View

Side View

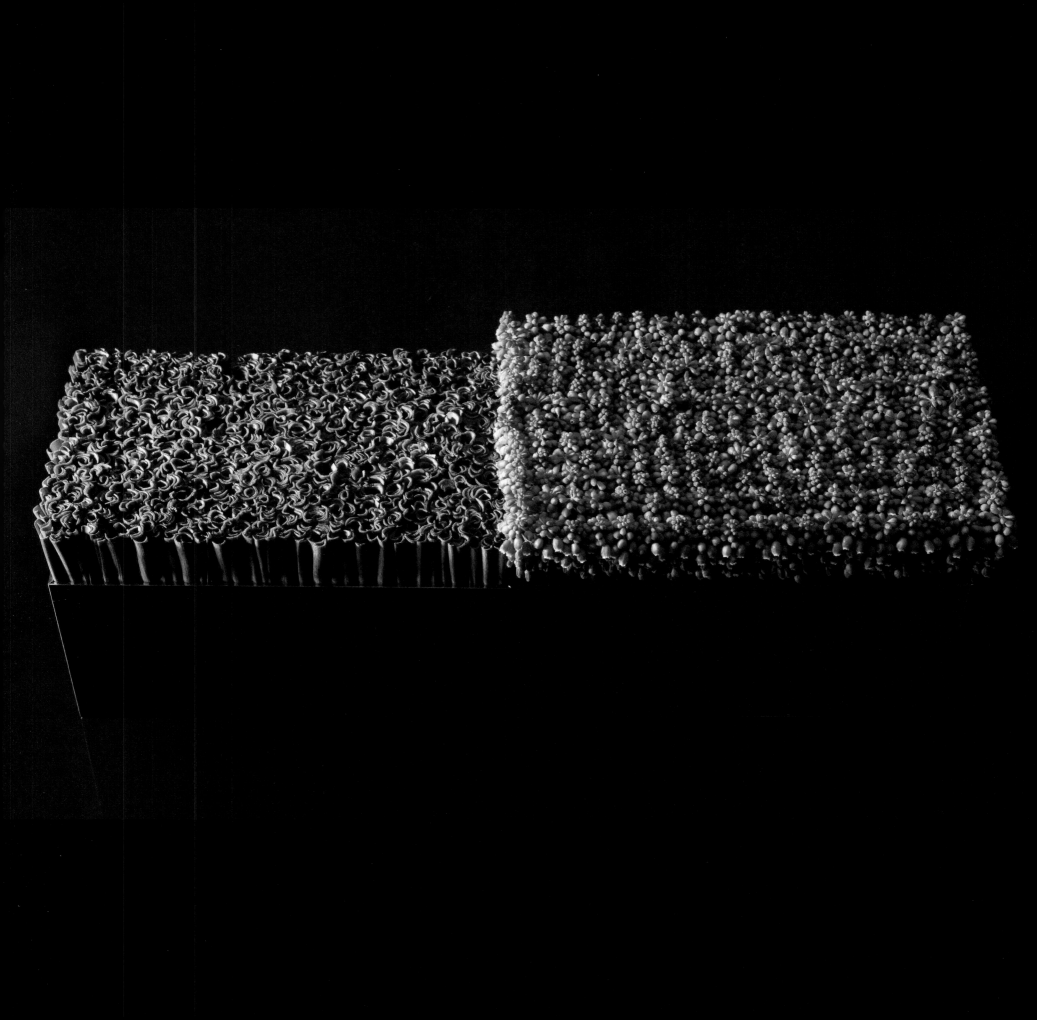

PRISM SHAPED ARRANGEMENT (LEAVES OF GRASS TREE, AMARYLLIS)

One leaf at a time, steel grass (leaves of the grass tree) is mounted on the sides of a quadrangular prism-shaped vase. The bases of the trapezoids forming the sides of the vase are different in size. Therefore, we carefully select appropriate steel grasses when working on the vase. If there is a narrow gap to fill in during the process, pointed ends of steel grass are cut even thinner with a knife to complete the project.

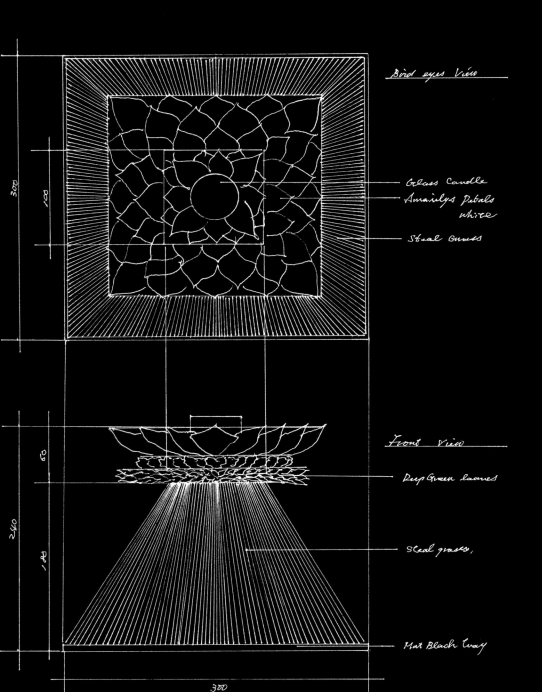

Bird eyes View

Glass Candle
Amarylys Petals
white
Steel Grass

Front View

Deep Green leaves

Steel grasses,

Mat Black tray

VASE MADE OF TRADITIONAL JAPANESE PAPER DYED WITH A KIMONO STENCIL

Traditional Japanese paper dyed with a kimono stencil passed down from the Edo-era was used for the vase of this arrangement. One single large sheet was made by layering multiple washi papers, and by hand small patterns were cut out on the surface. Even now, those patterns can be regarded as modern and therefore the flowers in the arrangement need to be in style and have an equally sharp outline.

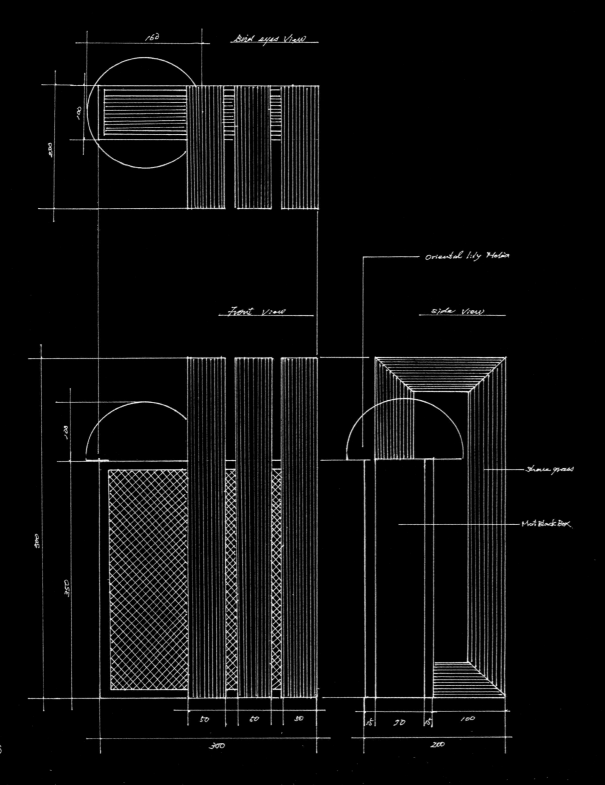

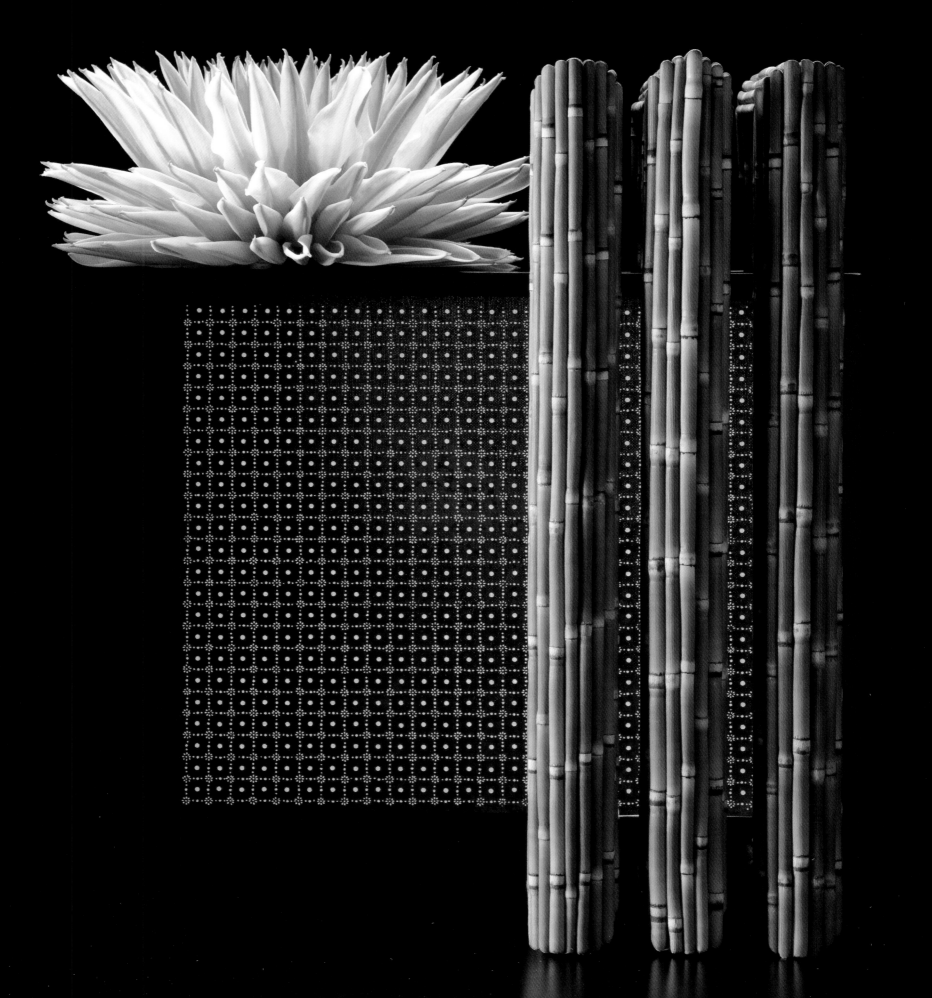

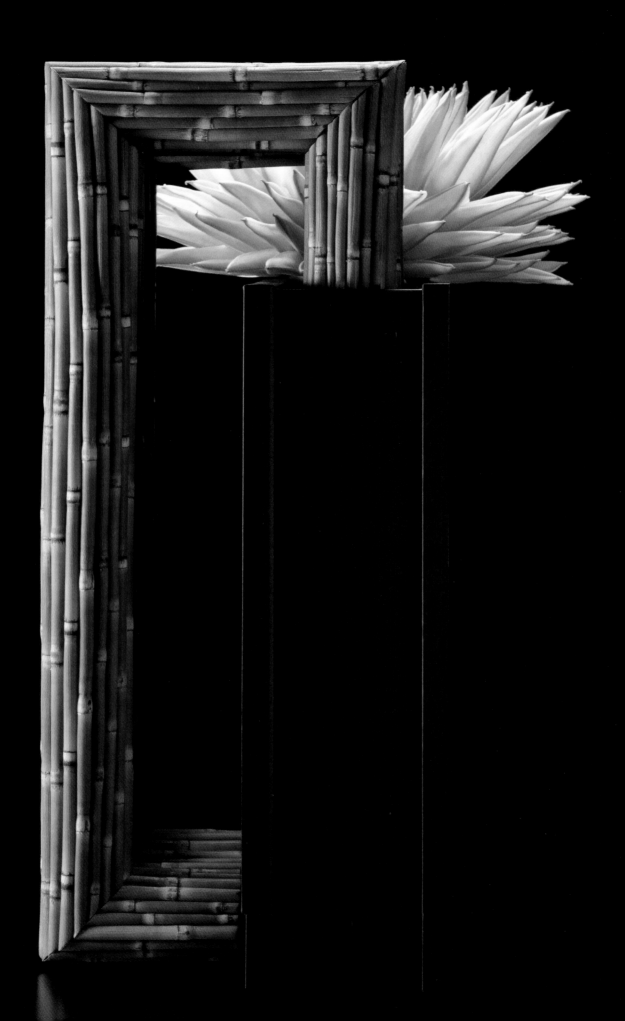

CYLINDRICAL

To create a beautiful cylindrical arrangement, be as simple as possible and avoid incorporating too many ideas in one design.

A contemporary impression can be achieved by using plant materials with long straight stems. Straight lines, although simple, give a strong and long lasting impression. Therefore we must not overuse this stilistic element, if used repeatedly on too many occasions it would weaken the effect. Bending the stems or focusing on different characteristics of the same flowers are alternative options to keep in mind. When a cylindrical figure is created with flowers or foliage, it is difficult to draw a precise outline of the arrangement. In such cases, we can come closer to a perfect cylindrical figure by highlighting the coexistence of the container and the plants.

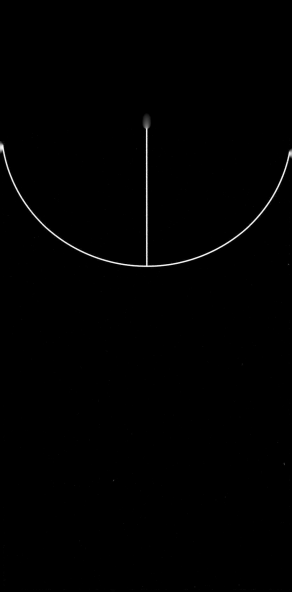

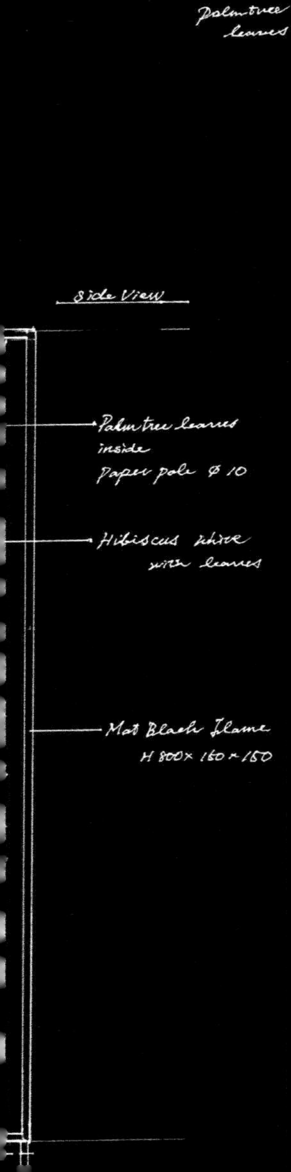

Palm tree
leaves

Side View

Palm tree leaves
inside
Paper pole ∅ 10

Hibiscus white
with leaves

Mat Black Flame
H 800 × 150 × 150

peppers are seperated from their branches and wired individually using traditional
nniques. The red peppers are pushed into a cylindrical piece of floral foam.
is gradually built up, working in stages from the top to the bottom. As each fruit is
he arrangement needs to be checked now and then, to make sure the outline and the
aintained.

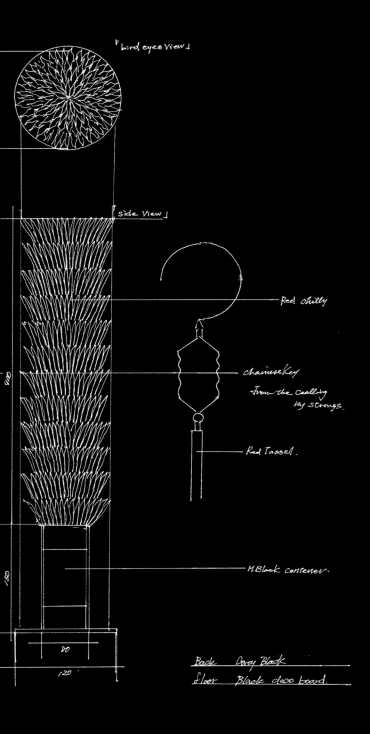

bird eyes View

Side View

Red chilly

chainese Key
From the Cealling
by strings.

Red Tassel.

H Black contener.

Back   Gray Black
floor   Black deco board.

CONTAINER MADE OF DRIED FLOWER STICKS (DAHLIA)

Sometimes we create containers for hotel suites using nothing but dried flower sticks. It is costly to prepare a new fresh floral arrangement every time guests stay. However, if an arrangement with only one flower in an attractive container is appealing enough, it reduces the expenditure without losing the effectiveness of the floral decoration.

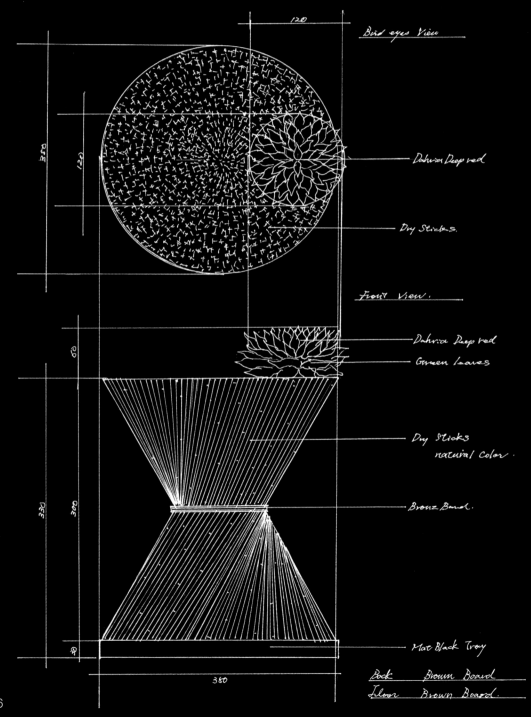

CURVACEOUSNESS

It is important to make the most of the beautifully shaped stems of calla lilies, especially when mixing them with other flowers in an arrangement. In this arrangement, the positioning of the roses should be well balanced, and, as the size of the rose circle affects the entire beauty, its length, width and its visual impact on the stems of the calla lilies should be thoroughly calculated in advance.

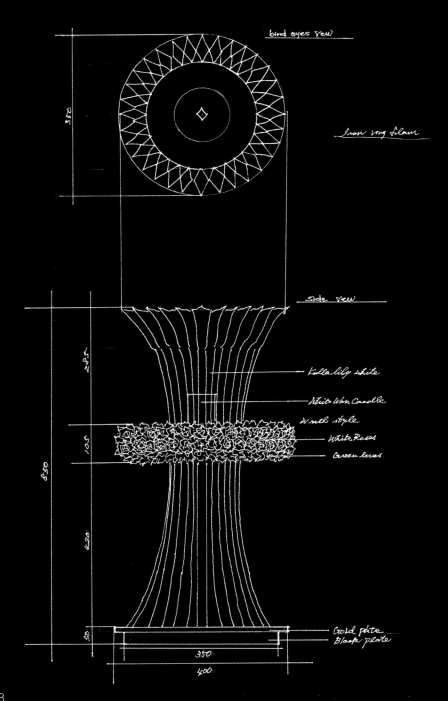

MIMOSA

The majority of yellow flowers are a pale pastel yellow and give a casual impression. The color of Mimosa flower heads however, is a vibrant bright yellow and gives an impression of depth. The reason behind this may be Mimosa's typical small flower heads, swelling and forming spherical clusters. I feel the yellow color and the absence of visible leaves could easily be an element of Japanese style.

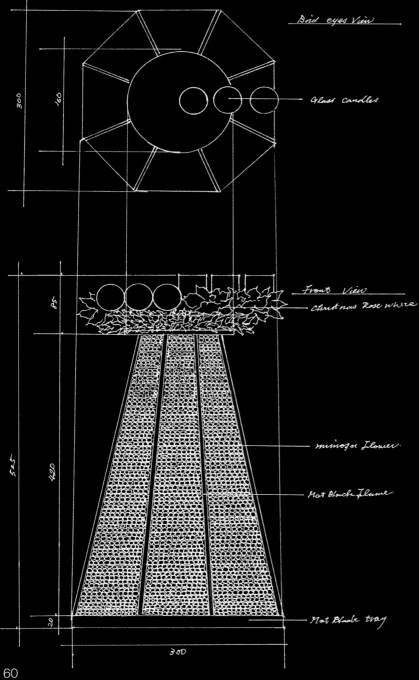

SHAPE OF JAPANESE ROYAL FERN (JAPANESE ROYAL FERN, WHEAT)

Japanese royal fern, a natural geometric figure, is one of my favorites. Until now I could not come up with any good idea to change its shape effectively to a superior one. Simple plants suit its naturalness better than gorgeous flowers, therefore I created this vase with nothing but regularly aligned wheat.

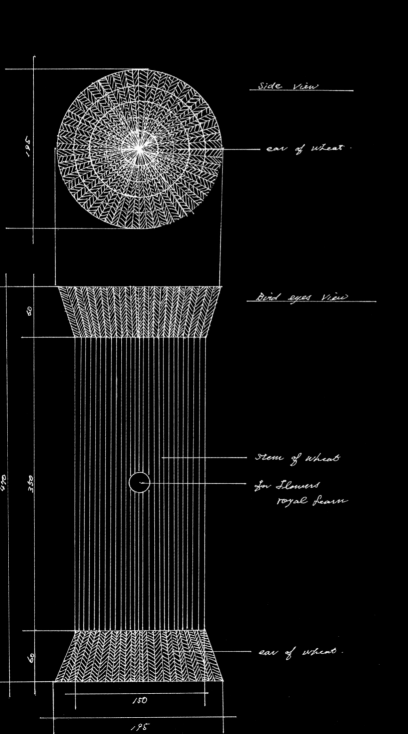

Side View

ear of wheat.

Bird eyes View

stem of wheat

for Flowers
royal fearn

ear of wheat.

196

60

470   350

60

150

195

IRIS OCHROLEUCA

The leaves of Iris ochroleuca, pistachio green thin leaves becoming narrower and more curved toward the pointed ends, resemble the edge of a Japanese sword. In arrangements they are usually placed with their wide, flat surfaces facing to the front, but here they are used showing their thin spine. The leaves are carefully aligned to draw the outline of this arrangement. When completed, the final shape is a cone, resulting from the leaves narrowing from the base to the pointed tip.

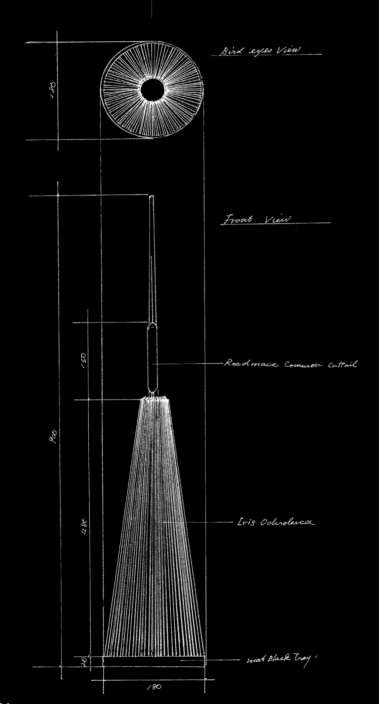

(RABAPPLE, NENINE)

rrangements that will bring an amused smile to t

ped with countless plumleaf crab apples, there is

iming at the apples. This unique device is likely t

K by Mieko Youki)

2 ⋅ ——

apples

nd lilais

——

apples.

and lily

and lily stems.

ain Tray φ180

Black & Art

Black.

BAMBOO CONTAINER (BAMBOO, JASMINE)

Before starting the arrangement, Moso bamboo is cleaved into long flat slices. The width of these slices is determined according to the size of the arrangement. All of them need to be equal in size. The pieces of bamboo are flexible and can be shaped into beautiful curved lines. Yet, they can be enormously stubborn and flex back. Therefore, stiff iron rings have to be at hand, to be placed above and below the basic mechanic to bind them.

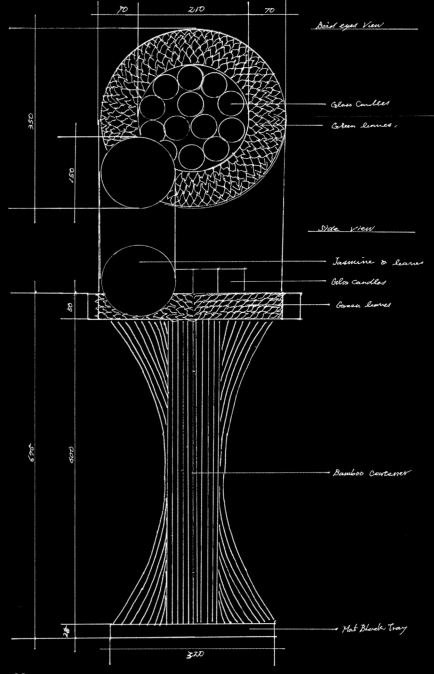

created for a wedding party held in Tokyo. Modern Japanese couples
mphasize their individuality and prefer their arrangements or decorations
icularly, the decorations for the guest tables are important and it is
unconventional and surprising as the floral decoration itself.

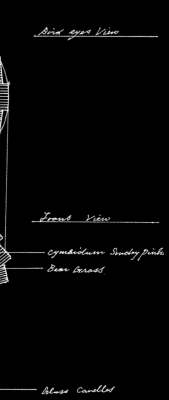

Bird eyes View

Front View

——— cymbidium Smoky pink
——— Bear Grass.

——— Glass Candles
——— Ball Chain Stand.

THREE-LAYER ARRANGEMENT (STAR-OF-BETHLEHEM)

This arrangement is structured by alternating layers made of stalks of Star-of-Bethlehem and layers of its flower heads, and ends with three layers of flower heads. The proportions between the thickness of the stalks and the size of the flower heads should be taken into consideration, since the flowers are used in full bloom. Each flower head is pointed upwards, making it clear that the general direction of this arrangement is upwards.

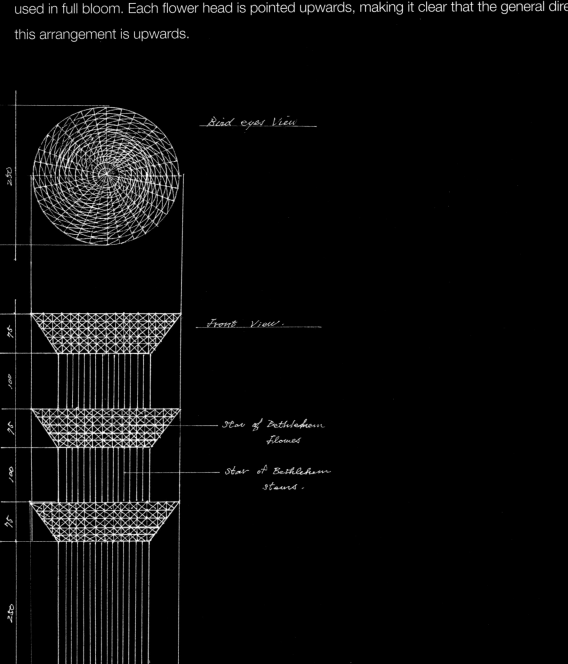

Bird eyes View

Front View.

Star of Bethlehem
Flowes

Star of Bethlehem
stems.

mat Black tray.

ave commissions for the floral decoration for parties held at Chinese

st cases, the clients wish that the party rooms are completely

hinese atmosphere. I used lychees, often served as a dessert in

or the vase. The lychees stacked in several layers intrigued the guests.

fabric
sh

Side View

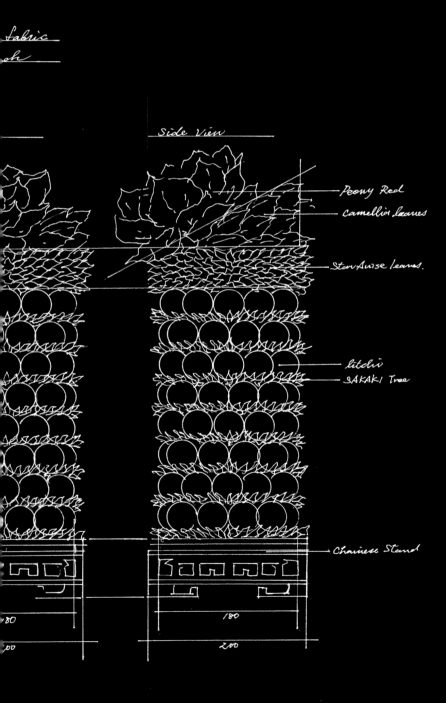

Peony Red

Camellia leaves

Star Anise leaves.

litchi

SAKAKI Tree

Chinese Stand

80

00

180

200

GREGARIOUS FLOWERS (CALLA LILY, GLASS CYLINDER)

The type of calla lily in pure white with a small flower head is fairly new on the market, but it has been and can be used on various occasions, including weddings. In an attempt to express the beauty of the pure white color and its continuity, it is more effective to create an arrangement with nothing but calla flower heads. Unlike the regular calla varieties, the stems are too thin and not very attractive on their own.

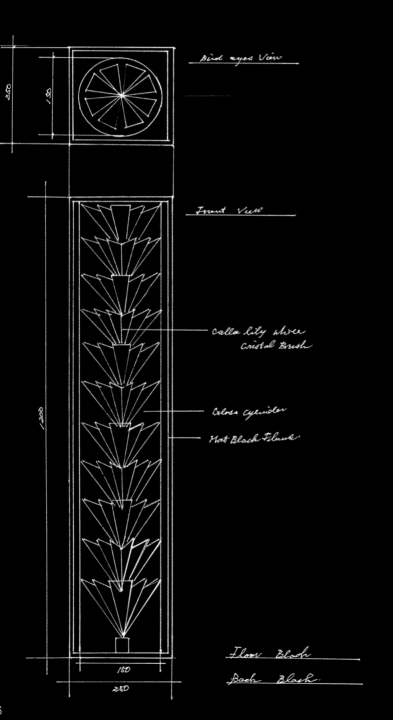

Bird eyes View

Front View

Calla lily white
Cristal Brush

Glass cylinder

Mat Black Film

Floor Black
Back Black.

TRIANGLE

Just like with SQUARE designs, making sharp
corners is a necessity when creating a triangular
arrangement. One of the difficulties to overcome
in triangular designs is adding a mechanic to
provide the plant materials with water. The choice
of method depends on the expected lifetime of
the design. In an event where the floral decoration
is supposed to last for only a short period of
time, using foliage could be effective enough to
keep the flowers fresh. But the rather bland look
of foliage could give the arrangement a plain
expression, something that can be avoided by
arranging one kind of foliage with 'in and out'
weaving technique for an accent or by using
foliage in different heights to form an extra motif
in the arrangement and achieve an even higher
degree of design. An arrangement shaped as an
inverted triangle appears most stylish hanging
from a wall or can be mounted on top of an iron
frame to achieve a floating look. This emphasizes
the tension and the sharpness of the pointed
ends.

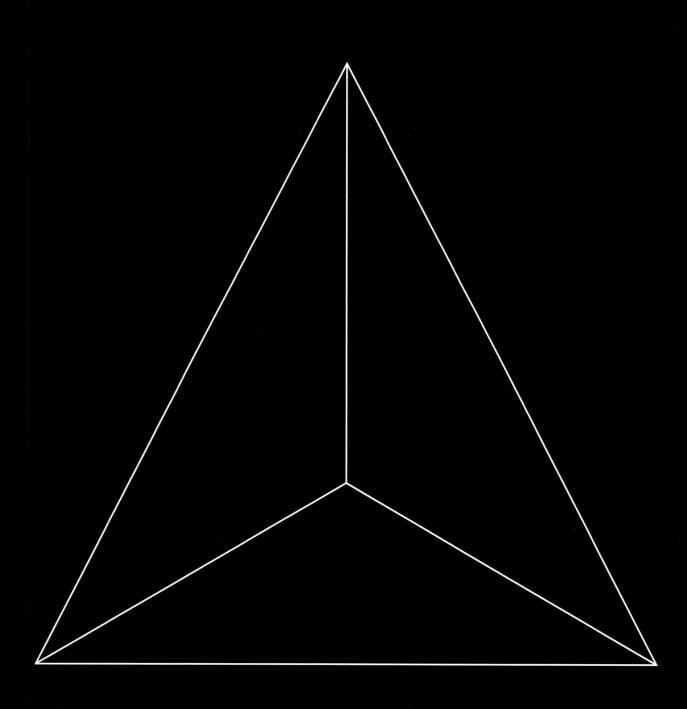

JAPANESE STYLE

The flat surfaces are made using bundles of lean, long steel grasses (the leaves of grass tree), and weaving them together, both horizontally and vertically. The finished work resembles a tatami (Japanese traditional straw matting) which is created in a similar way, but this one is made with Western material. One stem of passion flower or 'tokeiso' - in Japanese literally meaning 'clock flower' - appears as if it were ticking away the minutes. A design passing on the essence of the Japanese traditional flower arrangement.

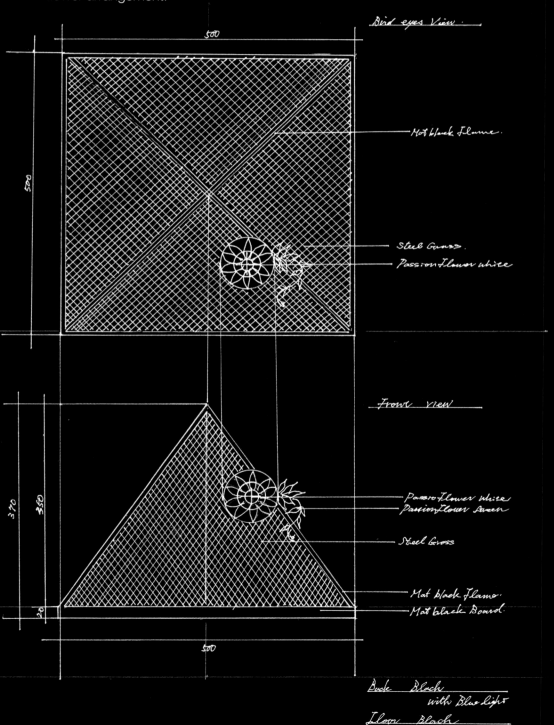

The great bulrush is a straight plant which grows in the Asian Far East and is frequently used in Ikebana.

I arrange them regularly and geometrically to make the diamond-shape more dynamic.

A single stem of Cattleya makes a nice contrast and appears like it is looming out of the arrangement

to communicate with us.

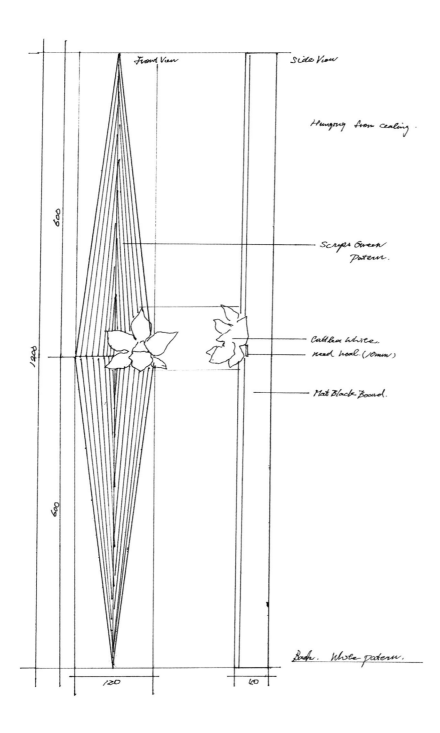

PLANT AND ART

'The Water Fall', an artwork by Nobuo Hashiba, expresses a stream of water falling down from high ground and its splash. It is composed with strips of white and platinum leaves on a bumpy clay surface plastered on canvas and shaped using his fingers. In front of this artwork, the umbrella plants, originally blooming at the waterside, stand straight just like the jet stream of a fountain. Plants and art sharing a common theme.

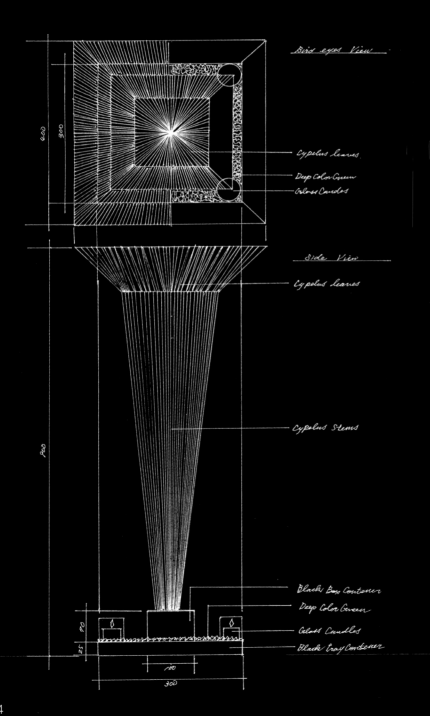

GREAT BURNET

Great Burnet, the wild grass that blooms in autumn, has numerous small brown fruits on every twig. The twigs are made into a fan-shaped figure by bringing all stems together in one point at the bottom of the vase and then gradually spreading them wider towards the top. Each stem is positioned with the greatest care, to avoid vagueness in the placement of the stems and the height of the heads.

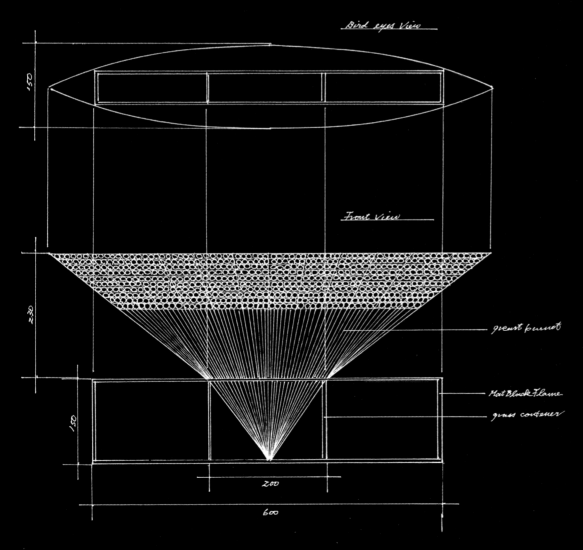

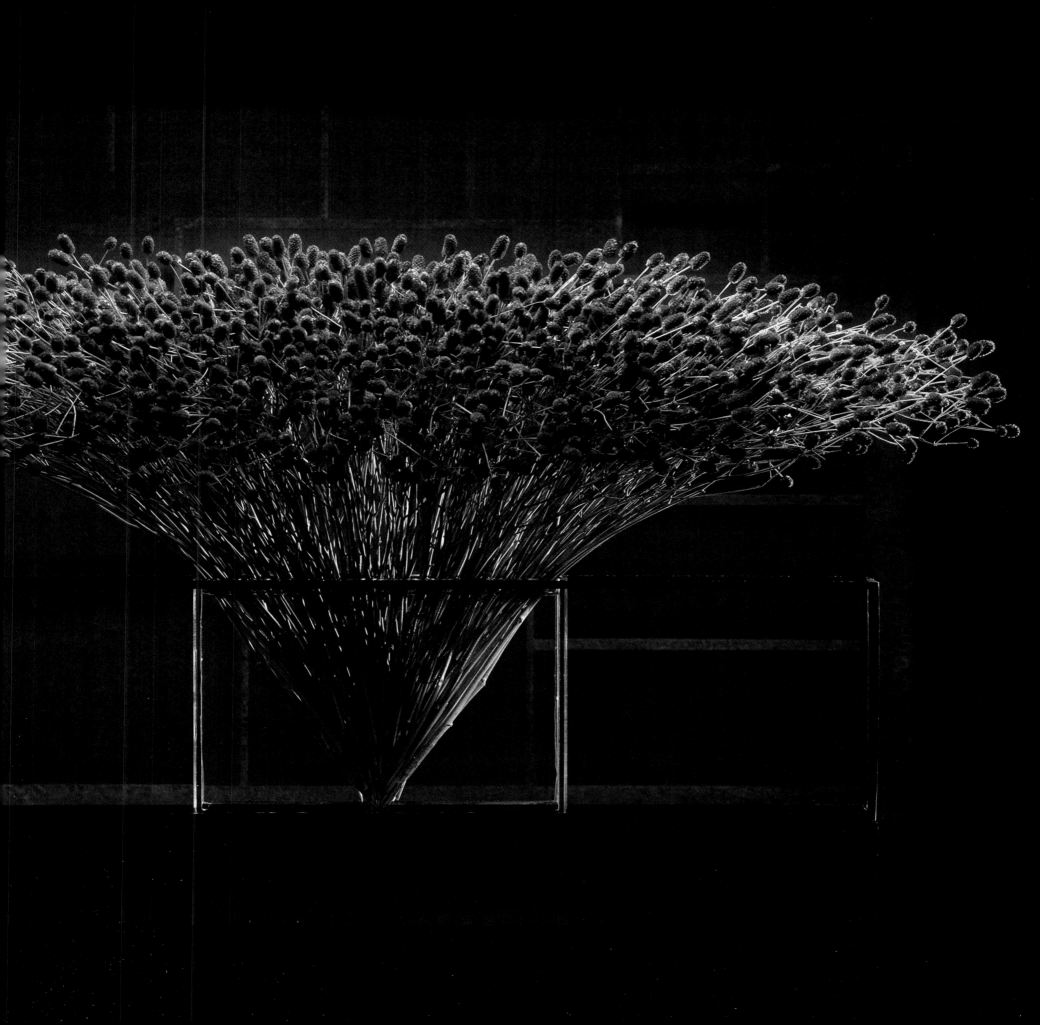

LOTUS

During summer, the lotus grows in water and reaches out to the sun to start flowering. To express the vitality of the lotus, several flower heads are stacked, a high towering stucture supported by a bundle of long lotus stems spreading widely at the bottom. The triangular shape of this arrangement enhances the impression that the lotus flower is trying to reach even higher to the sky.

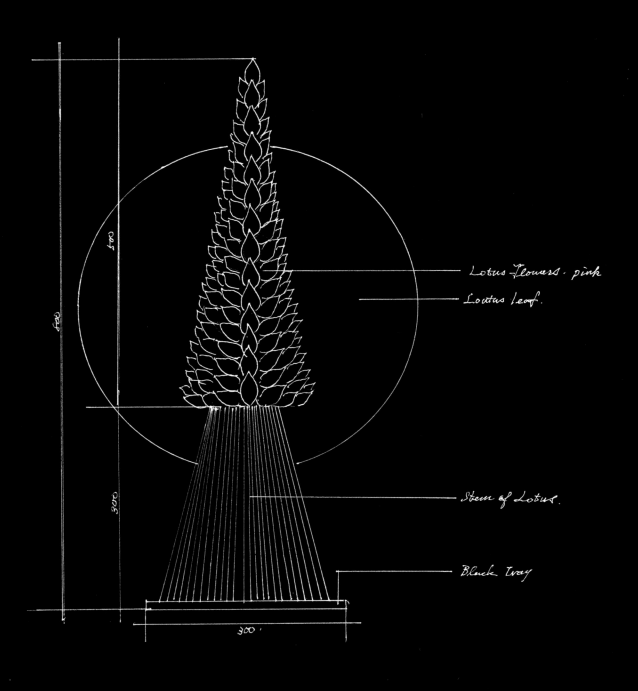

Lotus Flowers. pink

Loutus leaf.

Stem of Lotus.

Black Tray

Back   Brown Sable
Flower   Black Deco Bowl

CANDLE JUNE

Candle JUNE, a candle artist, is a peace activist who lights candles in Hiroshima, Ground Zero in New York and other sites to quietly remember the lost souls. His creation made of carved wax is both untamed and tranquil at the same time. Displayed together with the pine needles the candle creates a magnificent atmosphere, like the stone in a traditional Japanese zen garden (karesansui).

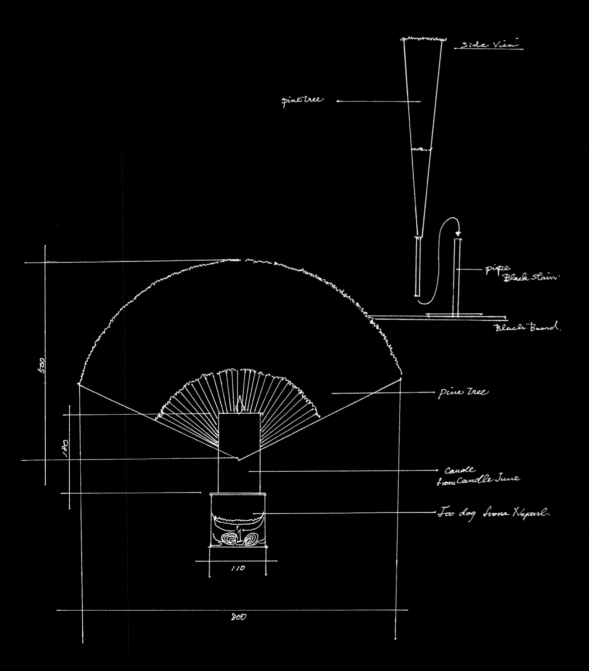

BAMBOO AND COMBINED FLOWER

A large triangular vase is created by cutting bamboo diagonally into several pieces and by joining them at the ends. Since bamboo gradually becomes thinner from bottom to top, only a small portion of a long bamboo stem can be used to assure that all pieces perfectly match in size. The joint and pointed ends of bamboo guarantee a very sharp and contemporary look.

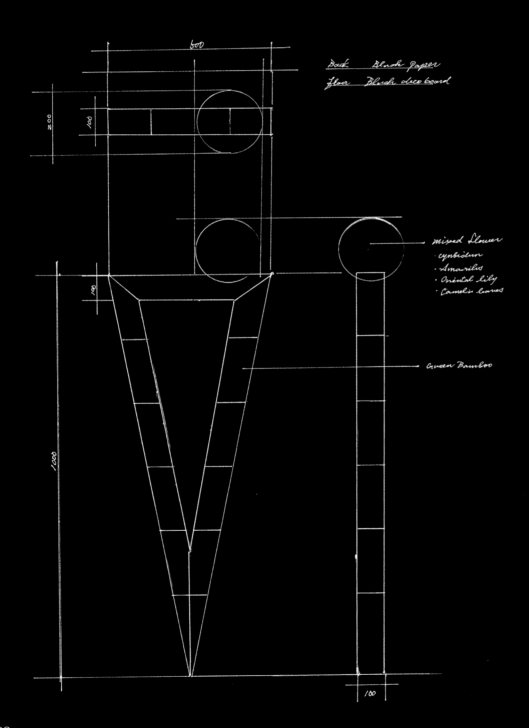

MADONNA LILY WHITE

The white lilies in the painting 'Annunciation' stand for the chastity of the Virgin Mary. The lilies behind the glass statue of the Virgin Mary* are arranged in a geometric formal style, with the tips of the petals perfectly aligned. The inverted triangular shape makes the flowers look smaller and assures the unification of the statue and the flowers.

*The statue of the Virgin Mary provided by Candle JUNE.

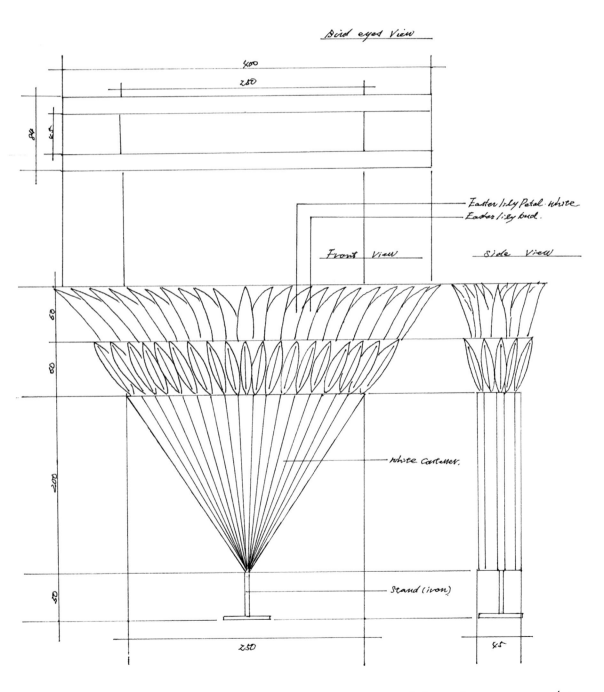

PINE

Pine tree is special for the Japanese. Being an evergreen it is a popular symbol of longevity. In old times, the warlords preferred to have many pine trees planted in the vicinity of their castle. It is believed that an entrance door decorated with pine drives away evil. We can still see it in the 'kadomatsu', a Japanese New Year ornament (a pair of auspicious pine and bamboo decorations in front of a house during the New Year period). On the surface of the art decorated with or next to the pine, messages to eliminate all evil are printed.

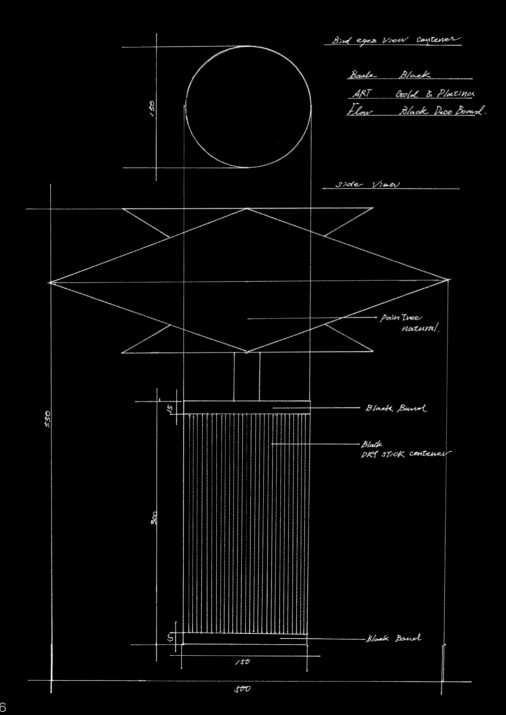

VERONICA

This arrangement is created with stems of Veronica, bundled tightly at the bottom and fanning out at the top. Naturally, the blue tips of Veronica are curved and not perfectly straight. This is overcome by wiring the flowering tips from top to bottom in a spiral. Having all tips standing upright makes the overall geometric shape sharper and even more convincing.

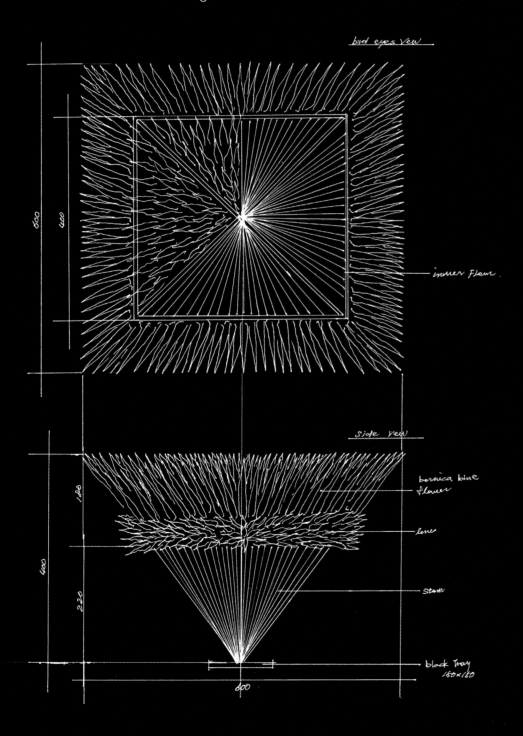

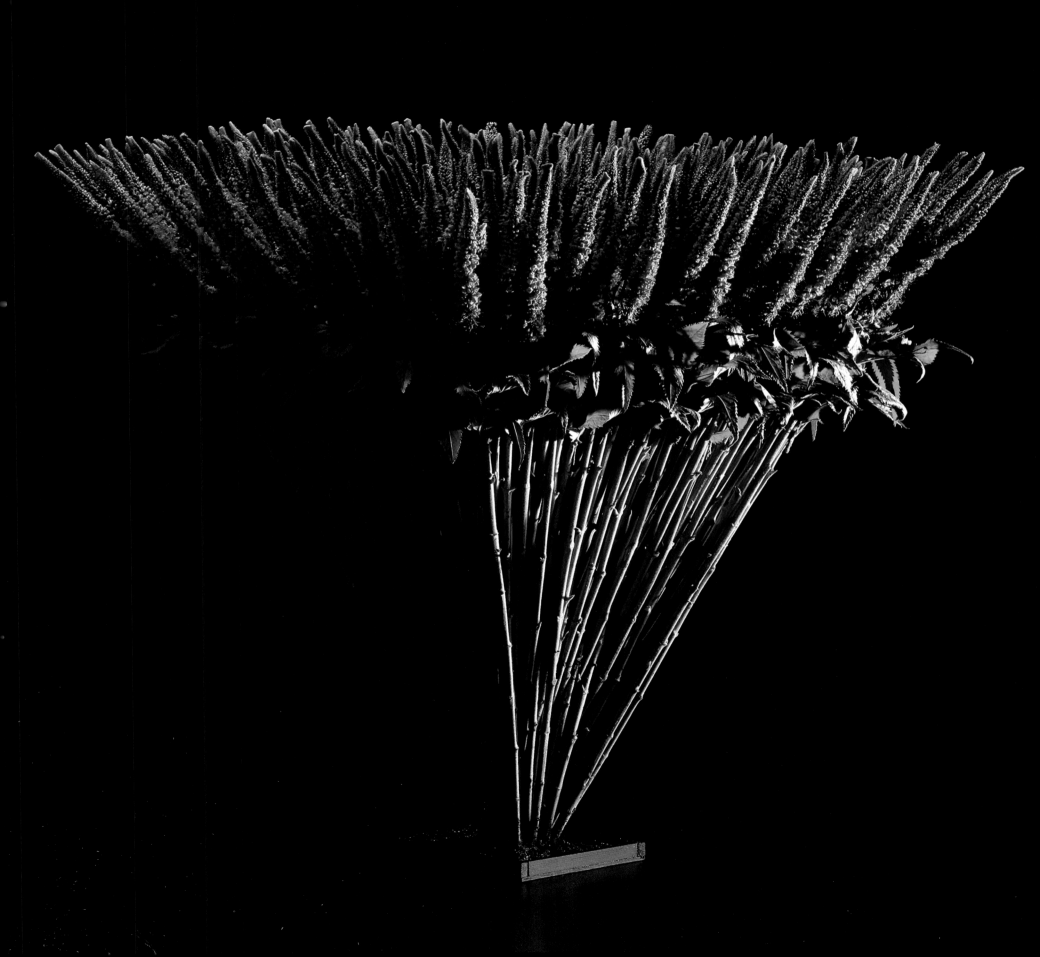

PEONY AND PLANTAIN LILY

Plantain lily has distinctive leaves, teardrop-shaped with sharp pointed ends and distinctive deep veins. Although the plant is not much taller than twenty centimeters, it gives a strong and stubborn impression. This arrangement is created by stacking the leaves gradually and topping the whole with a decorative white peony. Layered leaves of plantain lily look brave and dignified in a standing pose as if they were an armor of samurai.

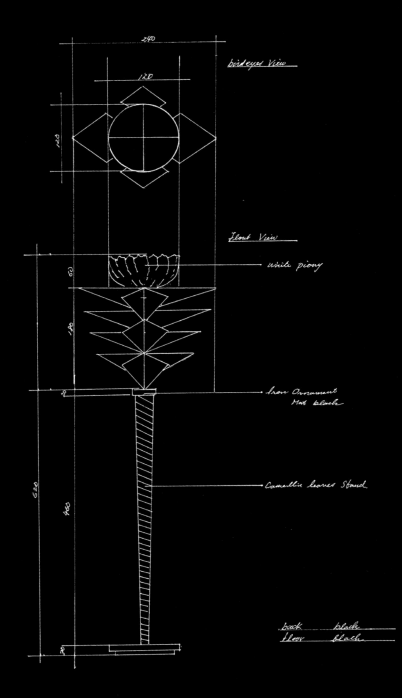

CANDELABRA

This modern candelabra in gold finish is an original made for a hotel in Sendai, the 'City of Trees', located in the northeast of Japan. The candles representing flower buds can be set at the pointed ends of the branches grown from the central part of the arrangement, representing a tree trunk. Using greenery or flowers with woody stems is most effective when arranging on a candelabra base

- Japanese Golden Bell Tree.
- Glass Candles Ivory
- Green leaves
- Black Tray 450x650
- Black Container 120x120
- Gold Tree Style Candi loveler
- Black Glass Cylinder

700

760

760

50

110

65

150

NIKE OF SAMOTHRACE AND ACANTHUS

When decorating with flowers, the relationship between the arrangement and the interior design is important. The space can have a very special ambiance and thus have special requirements for the floral decoration. The atmosphere of the time, the environment and the entire interior design concept have to be thought through carefully. Particularly for parties, suitable shapes and color schemes of arrangements, in accordance with the main party theme, should be determined in advance without a mistake.

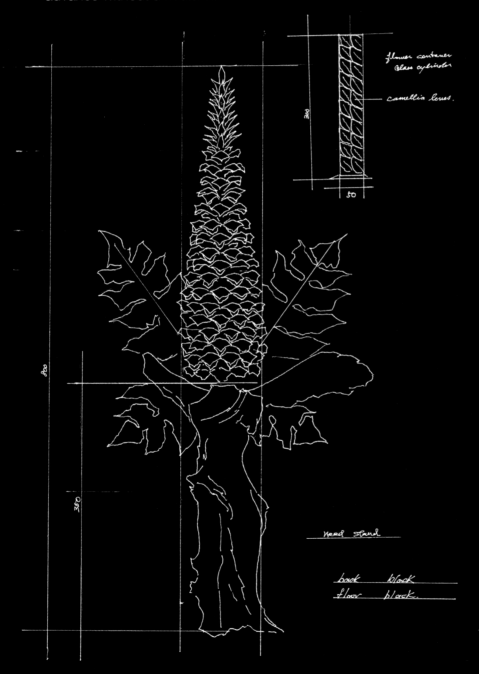

SUCCULENT PLANT

The silver, stainless steel, pyramidal vases were designed for the decoration of a modern Tokyo restaurant. Various kinds of succulents were chosen as plants for these arrangements. The shapes and colors of the succulents give a futuristic impression and suit the space and atmosphere of this restaurant very well.

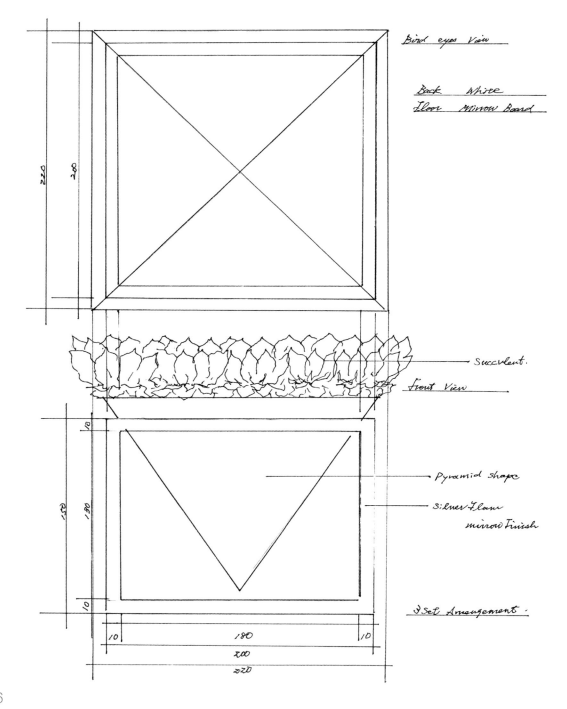

Bird eyes View

Back White
Floor Mirror Board

Succulent.
Front View

Pyramid shape

Silver Flam
mirror Finish

3 Set Arrangement.

FRUIT FLAVOR (CENTURY PLANT, RED CURRANT)

On the table for desserts at a party, varieties of lovely colorful sweets are displayed, making us cheerful just by looking at them. A floral decoration for that table needs to enhance the splendor of those desserts, therefore it is necessary to select a suitable material. In this arrangement, the attractive bright berries of red currant are perfectly ripe, as if they are just about to burst open, and glossy enough to be served on top of the desserts.

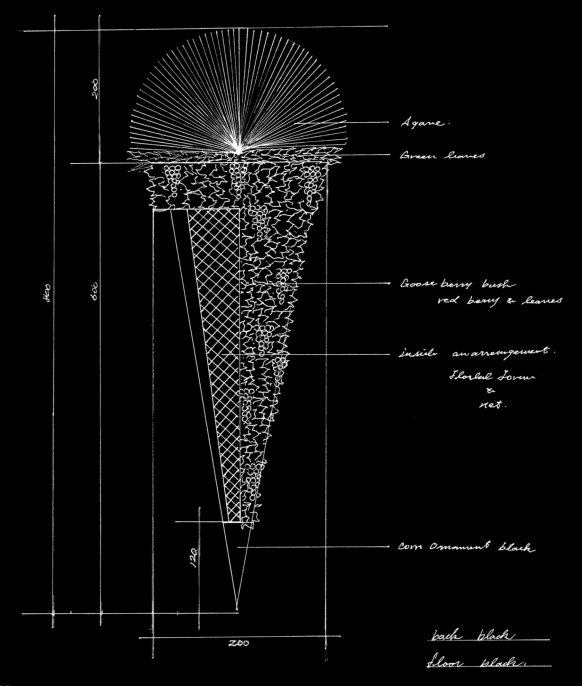

ranged in a triangular container floating on the water.
lar shape as convincing as possible, an appropriate amount
ely straight stems are to be selected during preparation.
nd shape of this arrangement is greatly affected by the
ds opening, this process must be controlled delicately by
ature prior to arranging.

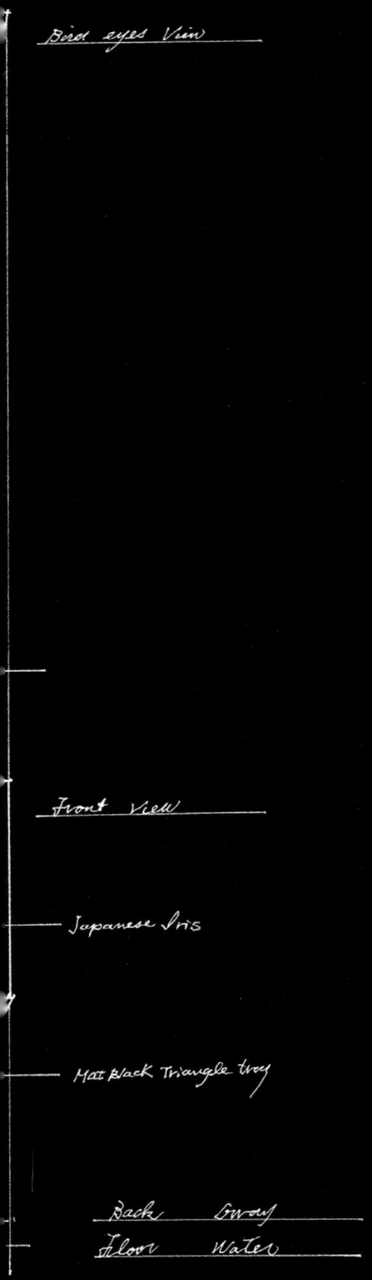

Bird eyes View

Front View

Japanese Iris

Mat Black Triangle tray

Back   Sway
Floor   Water

ROSE AND GLASS CYLINDER

Roses with varying stem lengths are individually dipped under water
in slender glass cylinders. Aligning the different containers visually gives us a
rhythmical, almost musical, impression. A good example of achieving a lasting
impression with a limited number of stems.

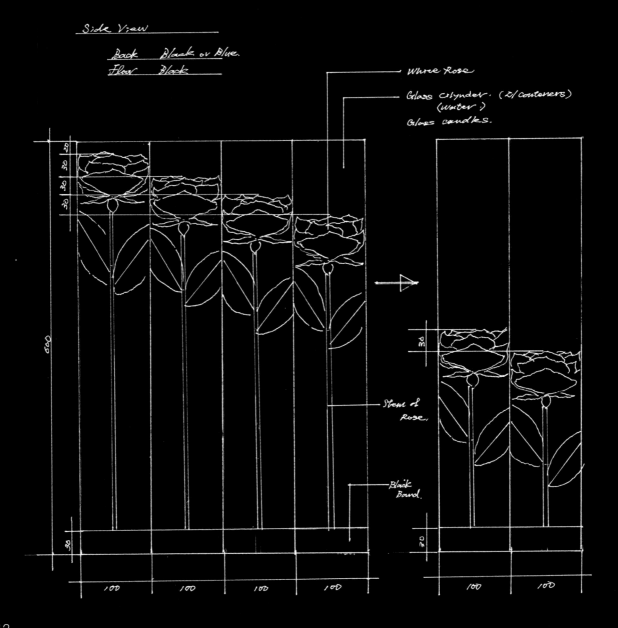

ROUND

Sphere-shaped and round arrangements have been popular in Europe since the old times. As we, the Japanese, have been influenced by European floral culture, the sphere-shaped style became very popular and it still is today. In a round arrangement, the positioning of the flowers at the base of the design is most important. Mostly, at the start of the design, the flowers are arranged in the shape of a triangle, but by adding more floral material and gradually arranging more densely, each 'spot' will become a 'flat surface' and will be transformed into a 'solid figure'. As the boundary between geometric formal arrangements and natural traditional arrangements is quite vague, we need to work very precise when moving on from 'spots' to a 'surface' in order to end with a design with a sharp outline.

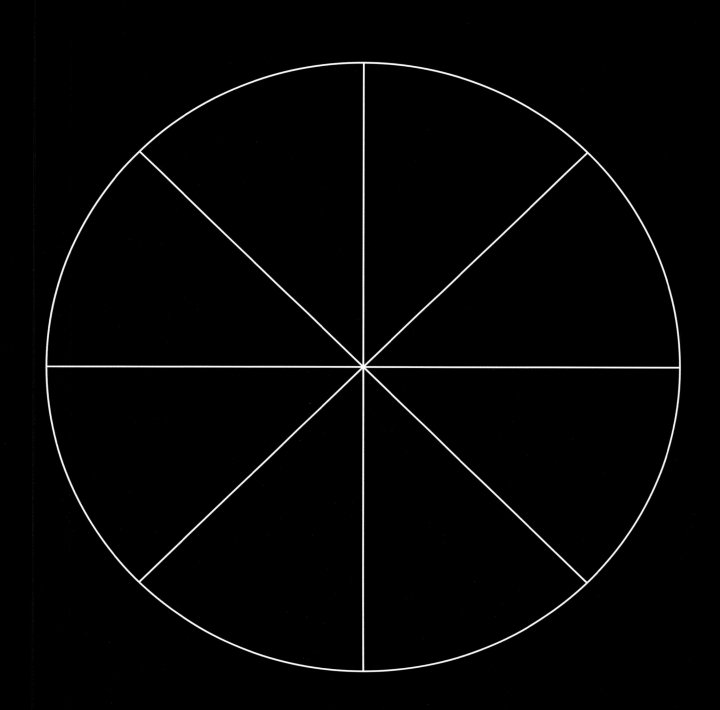

BULLET-SHAPED FOLIAGE (SLIPPER ORCHID, MING FERN)

Ming fern is a shrub with clustered small leaves and is often used in floral ar
at the joint the tiny individual leaves can be separated. Although ming fern i
formal arrangement, considering how the single leaves are small making it
figure, an enormous amount of leaves is required and designing with such s
time-consuming task. This work is curvilinear and bullet-shaped. A combina

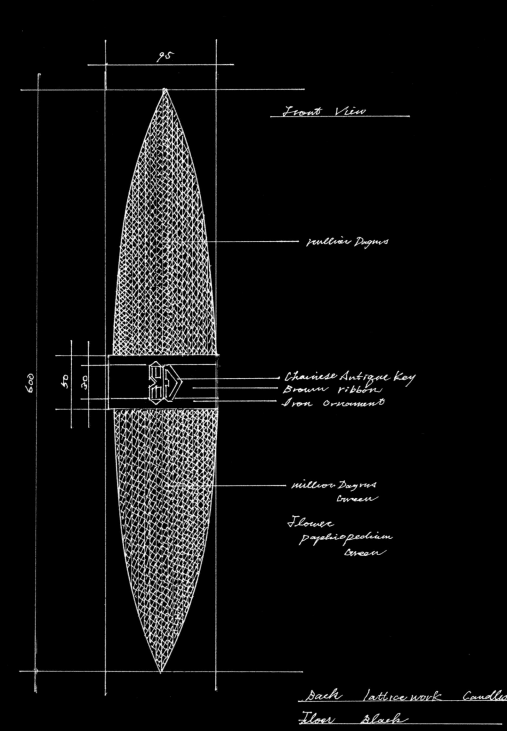

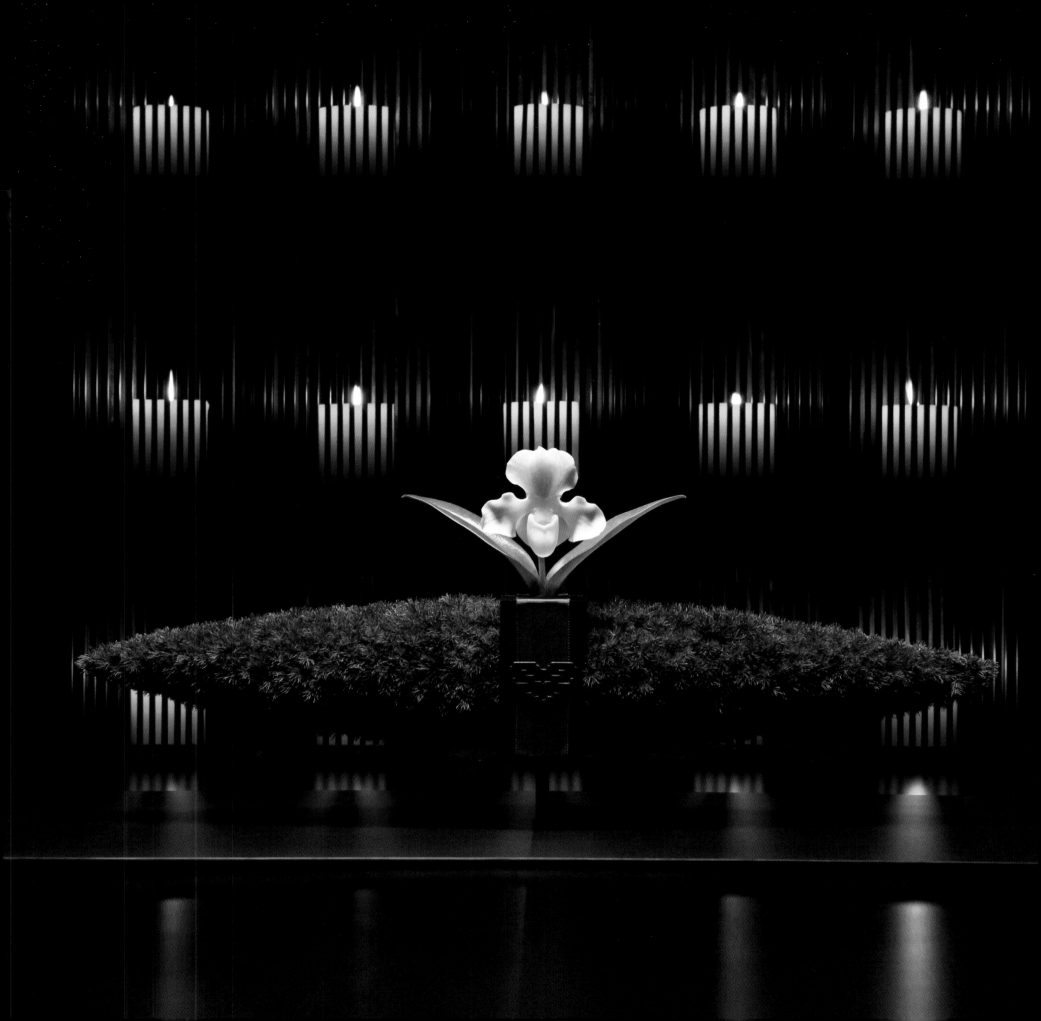

TWO-FACEDNESS OF SOUTHERN MAGNOLIA

Southern Magnolia is a tree which has not changed visually since the ancient times
and still survives today. The inside and outside surface of its leaves have different
colors and textures, which is one of this Magnolia's unique features. Green and
brown alternate randomly when using the leaves as a mass in a design. The two
faces of the Magnolia leaf give this simple sphere-shaped arrangement with just one
kind of plants an impression of depth.

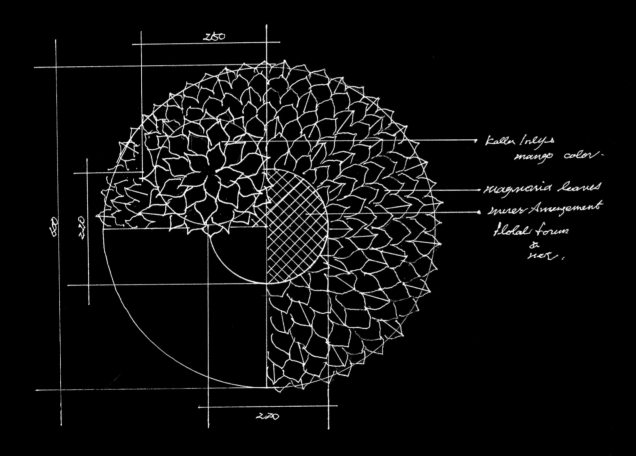

ARTICHOKE (ARTICHOKE, YUCCA)

Artichoke is native to the Mediterranean countries and frequently used as a food
ingredient as well. The oval shape, created by layering sharp pointed leaves of
Yucca, imitates the bud of an artichoke.

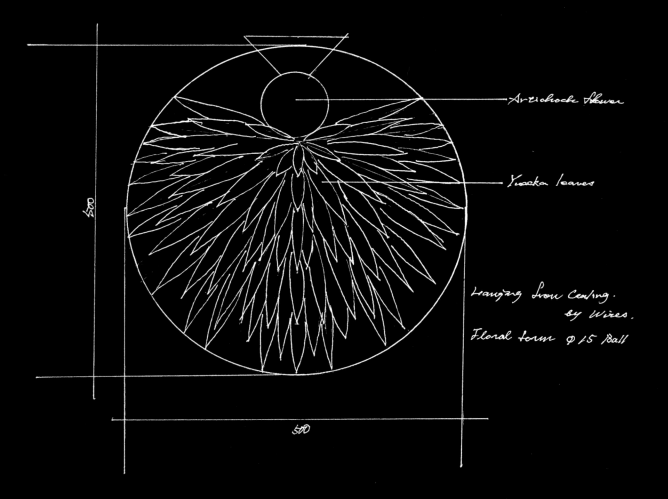

Side View

Artichoke flower

Yucca leaves

Hanging from Ceiling.
by Wires.
Floral form Ø 15 Ball

Back   White Board 3 steps
          & Blue light
Floor :white.

TROPICAL LEAF (JAPANESE BANANA LEAF)

Since the leaf of the Japanese banana plant has a strong individuality and a very distinct character it
is difficult to ignore its tropical image, no matter how we use it: in its natural shape, cut or modified.
However, as the leaf is flat and not too thick, it allows light to transcend through its surface, making
the veins stand out beautifully against the light green background when illuminated or submerged
under water. This is very striking when used for event or party decoration.

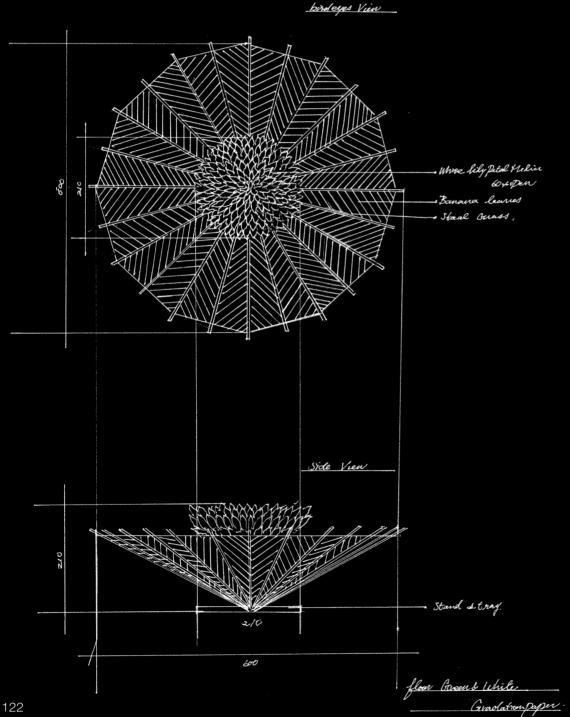

HYACINTH AND POPPY ANEMONE

The flower heads of hyacinths are removed from the stems, wired individually and arranged
in straight lines on the floral foam. Since the flowers are fairly equal in size, it is possible to draw
these lines quite accurately. Using different shades of blue for the top and sides clearly defines each
surface, making the end result more geometric.

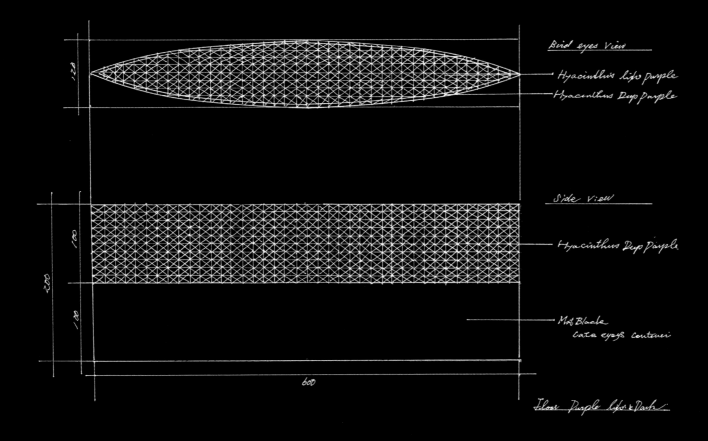

Bird eyes View

Hyacinthus lite purple
Hyacinthus Deep purple

Side View

Hyacinthus Deep Purple

Mat Black
Cats eyes container

Flower Purple light & Dark

Sakura (Japanese cherry tree) blossoms only for a fortnight in early spring. Soon after its moment of glory ends with petals scattered on the ground. We, Japanese, have a special relationship with the tree, as we tend to compare our lives and spirituality with it and more in particular with the way the blossoms flourish once and end suddenly but without regret. Keio-zakura used here is a species with small petals and a mass of blossoms on each branch, which is very convenient for this brilliant arrangement.

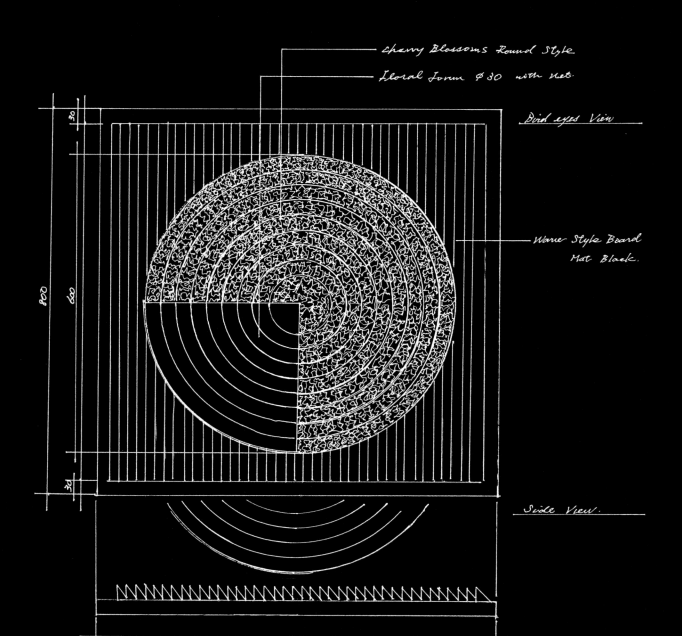

Cherry Blossoms Round Style

Floral Form ∅ 30 with net.

Bird eyes View

Wave Style Board
Mat Black.

Side View.

CYMBIDIUM ORCHID AND NEW ZEALAND FLAX

Plants will not come identical in size like machine-made products, not even when they are produced for the purpose. Although each flower or leaf may look exactly the same, closer inspection will reveal differences in size and subtle variations in color and other characteristics. In this work, New Zealand flaxes measured and cut accurately are placed along the outline of a circle and are later, after visual inspection, adjusted to achieve further preciseness and perfection.

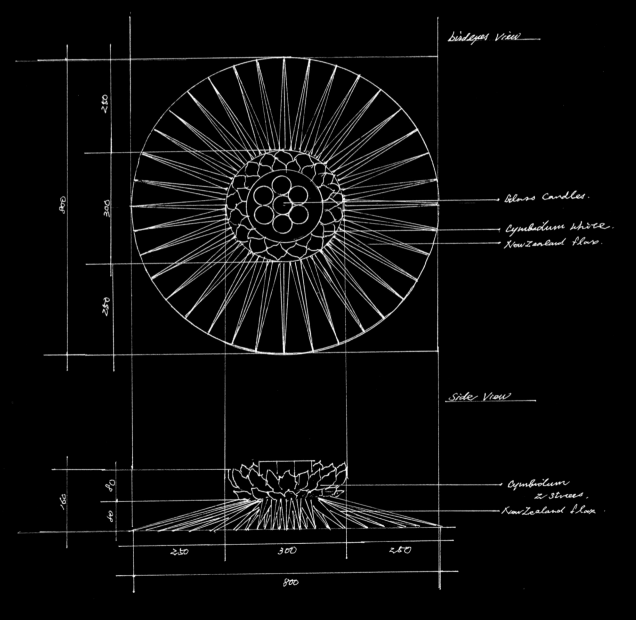

TULIP

It is said that there are several thousands of tulip species around the world. Many of them are available on the market today, and a wide variety of color schemes is possible. In particular deep purple tulips can be used in various styles of arrangements; elegant, modern or casual.

(Artwork provided by Nobuo Hashiba.)

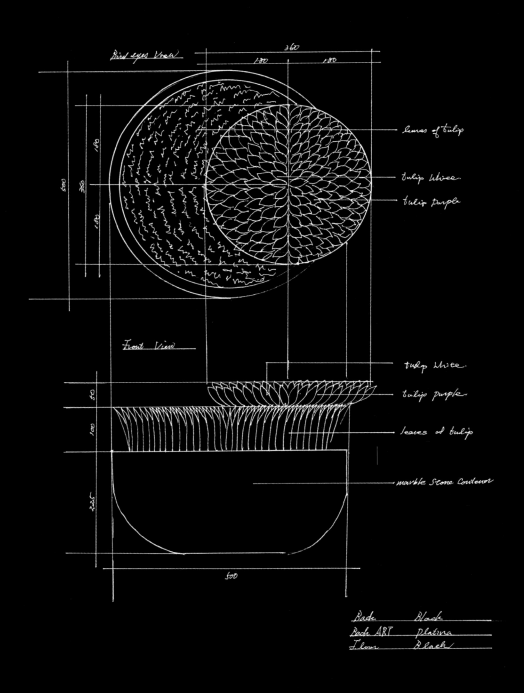

LILY-OF-THE-VALLEY

Lily-of-the-valley, which we see in early spring every year, is one of my favorites.
Therefore I have used them on many occasions, and have tried every technique
available. However they seem to be most beautiful when growing gregariously as
they naturally do. In order to enhance the prettiness of the flowers, the color and
shape of the leaves added to the arrangement, need to be considered carefully.

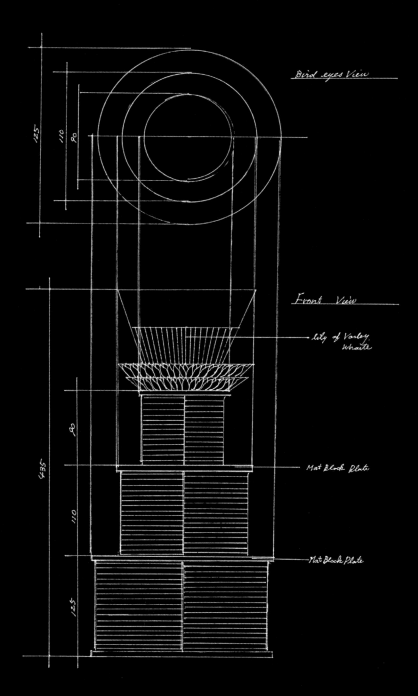

Bird eyes View

Front View

lily of Varley
Whaite

Mat Black Plate

Mat Black Plate

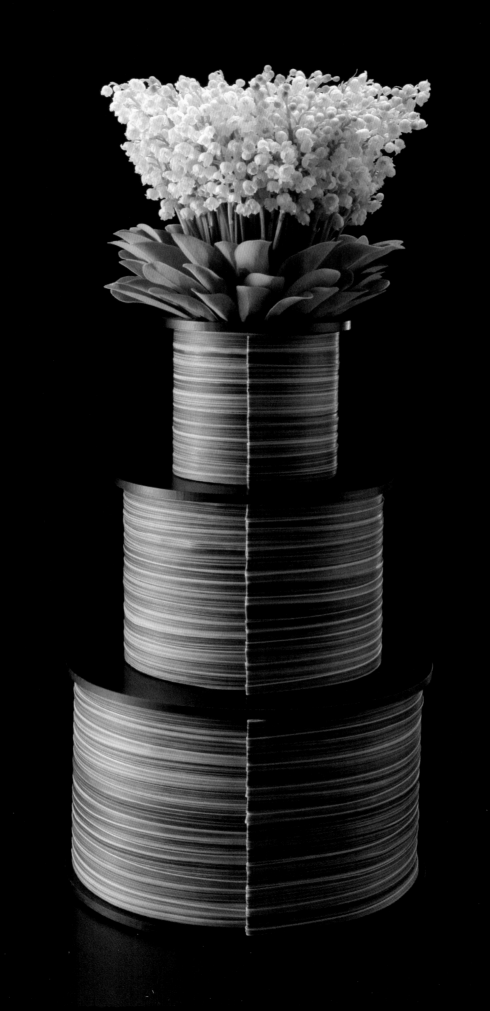

RECYCLED CANDLE

Candles are essential items in party decoration.
Combining them with flowers or incorporating
candles in a floral arrangement is becoming
a trend, and many florists have that in mind
when working. A sphere-shaped candle, fifty
centimeters in diameter, has great visual impact
just placed there without any additional devises,
and will remain in the viewer's memory.
This is a recycled candle, made by collecting used
candles from passed events. These are squashed
and melted in a mold. As a consumer of many
flowers and candles on various occasions, we
need to think eco-friendly and start acting as a
member and friend of the earth.

TETSUZO FUJITA

ACKNOWLEDGEMENTS

Reviewing this collection of my works in TOKYO FLOWERS, I realize that some readers may wonder whether these flowers truly reflect present Tokyo. However, considering that I have been involved in floral decorations for major hotels and parties hosted by famous fashion brand shops in this city, and have been invited by clients abroad as a 'Japanese' floral designer, I tell myself that it is probably acceptable to say that my floral designs represent a fragment of current Tokyo. We spent a year shooting these photos, and I regret that on some occasions we missed some seasonal plants. Looking at each design, I can vividly recall my emotional turmoil as well as the hardship and difficulties on the path to the finished arrangement. I still feel attached to every one of them.

Mr. Fuwa, the CEO of Plants Partner Co., Ltd. with whom I consulted before launching this project, gave me his approval immediately and provided us with abundant plant material throughout this year. In addition, Ms. Fumi Kimura, the chief editor of TOKYO FLOWERS, has been my guide since the very beginning of my career as a floral designer. From the time I struggled desperately to establish my own style to where I am today, she has always been a great mentor. Neither this book nor what I am today would have existed without these people, and I would like to take this opportunity to thank these two special persons.

I would also like to express my deepest gratitude to my staff for their cooperation, and those who supported me in various ways. I would truly appreciate it if I could continue to work with all of you, through my flower designs.

Yuji Kobayashi